BIMCO

Efficient ship management is an increasingly demanding task – operating in compliance with international rules at all times is crucial to avoiding challenges from port state controls and other issues that could delay your ship's operation.

BIMCO and Fathom's latest Guide gives a practical, guided approach for shipping companies – providing the right knowledge and tools to implement an environmental and efficiency management system.

The Guide is comprehensive but simple to use – its 'workbook' design gives a step-by-step approach to successful implementation – from building a corporate environment vision and commitment to change – to generating viable ideas and action steps at all operational levels from boardroom to ship.

Whether a company is taking the first steps to implementing an efficiency and environmental management culture – or looking for a clear, recognisable structure to document and drive activities already taking place, the guide has the right tools to help them achieve it. This approach also helps companies to see opportunities for improvements and cost savings more easily – and the steps towards putting them in place.

I recommend this guide to ship owners and operators as an excellent tool to facilitate the efficient management of ships, with steps to tackle the great and complex environmental challenges they face on a daily basis. It can also assist companies in minimising the risk of global non-compliance issues, which can be very costly and inconvenient for owners and operators.

John Denholm
President of BIMCO

ClassNK

Today, greater awareness of the need to protect the marine environment combined with commercial demands for greater efficiency are driving tremendous changes in our industry. Yet, adapting to constantly changing technologies whilst operating in line with tightening regional and international regulations presents a major challenge for stakeholders throughout the industry, especially for shipowners and operators.

As a leading classification society, we play a central role in the development and safe implementation of new technologies, developing and applying our own independent technical rules to ensure the safety of ships, their crews, and the marine environment, as well as working on behalf of more than 100 flag administrations to implement international conventions and regulations on vessels around the world.

Moreover, our surveyors carry out surveys and audits for more than 9,000 ships on our register each year. These vessels total more than 230 million gross tons or roughly 20% of the world's merchant tonnage under class, so we know first-hand the challenges that new regulations pose for shipowners and operators throughout the maritime industry.

Just as technology has advanced and become more sophisticated so too have maritime regulations. Beyond just grasping the requirements and intentions of these new rules, implementing new management policies, procedures, and best practices are essential to ensuring that compliance is achieved both effectively and cost-efficiently.

Any attempt to address the challenges of new regulations, however, must begin with understanding, and it is for that reason that we are proud to work alongside BIMCO to publish the Guide to Maritime Environmental & Efficiency Management.

This essential publication provides shipowners, operators, managers and charterers with a simple, easy-to-follow framework on how to efficiently manage vessels while keeping in line with safety and environmental rules and regulations. Moreover, the Guide provides simple steps on how to plan, implement, monitor and improve management systems in order to provide a competitive advantage whilst ensuring the protection of the marine environment and strict compliance with international conventions.

We believe that publications like this one will be of great benefit to owners and operators as they seek to achieve safe, effective and environmental friendly compliance. We are honoured to have supported the Guide's production; we salute BIMCO, Fathom, and Canada Steamship Lines for their incredible contributions to its contents, and we hope that you will find it a useful tool in your efforts to ensure safer and greener shipping.

387.5 AUS

The Guide to
Maritime Environmental &
Efficiency Management

Part One - The Framework

Authors: Catherine Austin and Isabelle Rojon

Expert Contribution and Review:
BIMCO Marine Department, coordinated by Jeppe Skovbakke Juhl
Dr. Anne-Marie Warris, Ecoreflect
Alison Jarabo, Fathom

Design: Ben Watkins

Published by: Fathom

Developed by:

BIMCO   fathom
marine | energy | environment

Supported by:

ClassNK

First published in 2015 by Fathom.

Copyright 2015 BIMCO and Fathom Eco-Efficiency Consultants Ltd.

ISBN: 978-0-9568259-7-1

CONTENTS

Part One - The Framework

FATHOM

The shipping industry is without a doubt influenced by growing societal pressure to take the impact of shipping operations on society and the environment into account. Cargo owners, charter companies, banks, investors and insurers are increasingly demanding evidence of environmental and operational efficiency commitments when making contract decisions. A greater awareness of the need to conduct shipping operations with environmental impact and ship efficiency in mind is becoming a necessity.

In an industry that is evolving and growing in complexity, developing awareness and acting strategically upon such awareness requires effective planning, foresight and long-term thinking, a structured approach is needed.

The structured approach required can be provided through the development and application of environmental management systems.

However, the number of environmental management systems currently available to the shipping industry are limited. Those that are available may be complex, not easy to follow and have not been tailored for application to shipping operations.

Fathom believes that ship owners and operators should have the correct tools available that will enable them to implement an effective management system and exploit all the benefits that are created through its development and application to create a lasting competitive advantage.

As information specialists, Fathom catalysed the creation of a resource that offers a practical, guided approach to support shipping companies on their path to establishing an environmental management framework that is tailored specifically for shipping operations to suit the unique requirements of the industry.

Whether you are taking the first steps to implementing an efficiency and environmental culture or looking for a clear structure to document and drive activities already taking place – this publication will provide you with the tools to help you achieve your goals.

Catherine Austin
Director - Fathom

CANADA STEAMSHIP LINES

Customers and communities around the world expect shipping companies to conduct their operations in a sustainable, efficient and environmentally-responsible manner. As part of a global movement toward sustainable business practices, the marine transportation sector is accountable not only to regulatory bodies, but also to the ecosystems and communities in which it operates.

The CSL Group ("CSL") a leading provider of marine dry bulk cargo handling and delivery services, and the world's largest owner and operator of self-unloading vessels, strongly believes shipping companies must take a proactive approach to promote technologies, solutions and sound public policy to reduce the industry's environmental impact. In the past few years, CSL has made remarkable progress to improve the energy efficiency and environmental performance of its global fleet. In fact, environmental stewardship has become a natural extension of CSL's collective consciousness.

CSL is a leading advocate of short sea shipping, a critical segment of global trade and a significant contributor to reducing the environmental footprint associated with transporting large quantities of bulk cargo. Typically operating along coastlines and rarely transiting vast ocean distances, short sea ships play a key role in reducing greenhouse gas emissions, noise and congestion problems by competing directly with less efficient transportation modes such as truck and rail.

Despite its inherent economic and environmental advantages, short sea shipping is often overlooked by governments, and must comply with inadequate global regulatory requirements designed for deep sea shipping. The unintentional consequence is a modal shift to less efficient forms of transporting bulk cargo.

As part of a global solution to move cargo in an efficient and environmentally-responsible manner, short sea shipping must be defined, defended and promoted to support a viable and sustainable shipping industry. CSL is actively working to ensure short sea shipping is accorded an internationally recognized definition, with sound policy development and proper convention negotiation.

CSL is honoured to have participated in the development of the 'Guide to Maritime Environmental & Efficiency Management', in collaboration with BIMCO and Fathom. We hope the insight and knowledge contained in the guide will enhance the environmental management of shipping around the world and lead to global improvements in fleet efficiency.

CANADA STEAMSHIP LINES

ABBREVIATIONS

The abbreviations listed are solely for Part One of this Guide.

Abbreviation	Meaning
CMS	Compliance Management System
ECP	Environmental Compliance Plan
IMO	International Maritime Organization
ISM Code	International Safety Management Code
ISO	International Organization for Standardization
MARPOL Convention	International Convention for the Prevention of Pollution from Ships
MOU	Memorandum of Understanding
PSC	Port State Control
SEEMP	Ship Energy Efficiency Management Plan
SMS	Safety Management System
SOLAS Convention	International Convention for the Safety of Life at Sea
USCG	United States Coast Guard
US DoJ	United States Department of Justice

CHAPTER ONE

CONTENTS

THE GUIDE TO THE GUIDE

THE GUIDE TO THE GUIDE

This Guide offers practical guidance and resources that will equip you with the knowledge and tools to develop and implement an organisation-specific environmental and efficiency management system. The aim is to help you improve your environmental performance, improve the efficiency of your ships and fleet - and therefore remain competitive in the changing business landscape.

This Guide is presented in three different parts.

1.1 Part One - The Framework

Part One provides guidance on how to develop an organisation- and maritime-specific environmental and efficiency management system, referred to throughout this Guide as the Environmental & Efficiency Management Framework. It will assist you in developing and implementing a management system in an easy way and exploit the benefits that stem from it to create a lasting competitive advantage.

The fundamental idea behind building your Framework is to use a modular approach. This will allow you to adapt your Framework to your organisation's specific needs and circumstances, link it to an existing management system or facilitate the development of a full management system.

In addition, Part One demonstrates how this resource and your resulting Framework links to other industry requirements, including the International Safety Management (ISM) Code and the Ship Energy Efficiency Management Plan (SEEMP). Your Framework can also be used to help deal with US enforcement action where the development and implementation of an Environmental Compliance Plan (ECP) can be imposed on a company. Part One also explains how your Framework relates to standards developed by the International Organization for Standardization (ISO), such as the Environmental Management Standard ISO 14001 and how it can be used to participate in the most common environmental evaluation schemes.

1.2 Part Two - The Handbook

Part Two is a compendium of technical and regulatory information, advisory resources and templates - the technical counterpart to Part One. It covers the entire spectrum of environmental issues related to ship operations, including:

- Oil pollution.
- Garbage.
- Sewage.
- Chemical pollution.
- Air pollution.
- Ballast water.
- Biofouling.
- Underwater noise.

Each Chapter within Part Two provides a brief introduction to each issue, explains what the associated environmental impacts are and describes related international and regional regulatory requirements. Each chapter also covers how your organisation can not only meet and comply with these regulatory requirements but move beyond them. Each Chapter also presents the potential business case for measuring your organisation's environmental performance.

1.3 Part Three - The Templates

The Maritime Environmental & Efficiency Templates (on the USB memory stick supplied) are an extensive library of templates in the form of logbooks, forms and data collection tools that supplement Part Two of this Guide.

Together, the three parts provide an essential resource that will support your organisation in developing an effective Environmental & Efficiency Management Framework that is specific to your organisation and operations and can be adapted to changing circumstances.

CHAPTER TWO

CONTENTS

THE ENVIRONMENTAL & EFFICIENCY MANAGEMENT FRAMEWORK

THE ENVIRONMENTAL & EFFICIENCY MANAGEMENT FRAMEWORK

2.1 What Is Your Framework?

The Environmental & Efficiency Management Framework has been developed to equip your organisation with the resources, practical tools and information needed to develop and enhance your organisation's management of environmental and efficiency issues. It is tailored for application within the maritime industry and can be moulded to fit your organisation's specific needs.

Building this Framework for your organisation (from herein referred to as 'your Framework') will be principally carried out in your shore-based office, with support from ships' crews as relevant. The active operation of your Framework, on the other hand, will be a joint assignment with shared responsibility between shore and ship-based staff.

This resource assumes that shore-based staff only have limited experience with establishing such a Framework and that the individuals assigned to building it may only be able to dedicate limited amount of their time to this undertaking. However, this resource is similarly useful for staff or a team that hold varying levels of experience in this field, or are dedicated to working on the development of the Framework full time.

Please note that this resource does not impose any requirements on your organisation. Instead, your organisation can decide which requirements it wants to fulfil or go beyond, e.g. Ship Energy Efficiency Management Plan (SEEMP), International Safety Management (ISM) Code, ISO 14001, ISO 5001, etc. As you build your Framework, please ensure that any requirements your organisation wishes to fulfil are incorporated into your Framework and that the language, terms, processes and information used in your Framework match those required.

2.2 The Guiding Principles Of Your Framework

The development of your Framework will involve undertaking tasks that are specific to your organisation's needs. However, there are a few guiding principles that underlie all your development tasks and that should be kept in mind as you develop your Framework.

2.2.1 Iteration Is Key

Building your Framework is not a linear process, but an iterative one. This allows you to focus on issues where your organisation most needs the support of a Framework. It also allows you to learn from previous experience and feed new knowledge back into the development of your Framework.

The journey to developing your Framework is unique to your organisation, its needs and intentions for your Framework and its timelines. Your Framework will be dynamic and constantly evolving.

The advantage of an iterative process is that it allows you to extend the development to where you most need it.

2.2.2 Respect Your Reality And Culture

Each organisation is unique. In order to develop and operate your Framework successfully, you need to respect your organisation's reality – including its current circumstances, culture, staffing and resources - and ensure that your Framework integrates successfully with your organisation's unique situation.

2.2.3 Commercial Benefit Must Be Priority

Always keep in mind that your Framework is meant to support your organisation. Building your Framework is about balancing commercial practicality with viable and informed choices related to environmental and efficiency issues so as to enhance your organisation's commercial success.

To ensure this, keep business benefits in mind when carrying out the various tasks to build your Framework.

2.2.4 Keep It Simple

Base your Framework upon simple language to explain processes and use the simplest approaches to achieving your organisation's needs. Remember that these are often equally or more effective than more complex ones. This will help you develop a realistic Framework that can be put into practice at a reasonable pace.

2.2.5 Keep It Focused

The core focus of your Framework is on managing environmental and efficiency issues.

All suggestions or actions related to your Framework only apply to environmental or efficiency issues, so if a subject appears to be very broad and does not in any way relate to these issues, dismiss it.

2.3 How To Build Your Framework

This resource has been developed in a manner that advises simplicity while recognising that building your Framework will not happen overnight as it involves varying tasks that demand specific timeframes and feedback mechanisms.

The idea behind this resource is to provide a set of building blocks that you use as you need them. It takes a modular approach allowing you to link various elements of your Framework to an existing management system or facilitating, in principle, the development of a full environmental management system.

Some tasks build on others, meaning that they will be easier to complete with the knowledge and insight gained from previous tasks. To help you navigate and quickly identify those previous tasks, a figure of building blocks next to a task shows which other tasks should be completed beforehand.

Whilst navigating this Guide, please remember no Framework will be the same and it may even vary between ships in the same fleet. Please use those parts of this resource that you find useful and that can make a difference to your organisation.

2.3.1 The Four Areas

Building your Framework involves a number of tasks.

These tasks can be broadly grouped under four different areas:

- Scoping where you are as an organisation and planning where you want to be.
- Organising how to get to where your organisation wants to be.
- Tracking your progress and safeguarding where your organisation wants to be.
- Ensuring your Framework stays on track, refining processes and maintaining momentum.

Throughout this chapter, simplified terms that represent the four areas described above will be used to form a tagging and tracking system through which you can easily identify your position within the four areas.

The simplified terms for the four areas are:

- Scoping & Planning.
- Organising Your Approach.
- Safeguarding Your Progress.
- Staying On Track.

2.3.2 Considering Varying Complexity

Building a complete Framework requires the execution of a number of tasks.

When considering how to tackle the tasks, the choice you face is to either:

- Complete ALL of the tasks in an area in full before you move on to the next area; or
- complete SOME of the tasks in an area before moving on to the next area to allow you to see the outline of your Framework and test what works and what does not.

Additionally, your organisation can choose which activities to include in its Framework. Again, the choice that you face is to either:

- Include all activities as you begin a task within an area; or
- choose to include some activities or just one activity, adding others later as you progress, learn and figure out what works well for your organisation.

This resource is presented assuming that you have a preference for undertaking some tasks within an area and moving onto the next area. Also the assumption is that you will initiate the development of your Framework with some but not all activities that you wish to include in your final Framework. You can continuously go back to previous tasks, adjust and add to them, as required.

For this reason, the four areas (see 2.3.1 for the list of the four areas) have been divided into 'Starting' and 'Advancing' tasks:

- **Starting Tasks** allow your organisation to initiate the development of your Framework by picking those tasks applicable to your organisation's specific situation.
- **Advancing Tasks** allow your organisation to add more detail, depth and complexity to your Framework, should you want to.

In keeping with the principle of your Framework being an iterative system, you will be returning to review your tasks and activities as time goes by.

Should you wish to build your Framework by completing all the tasks within an area fully before moving on to the next area, you should complete the Advancing Task after you complete the Starting Task, in addition to including all the activities you wish your final Framework to include.

It is a case of: your Framework, your rules! Keep it simple, achievable and applicable to your organisation.

2.3.3 Starting And Advancing Tasks - The Format Explained
This resource assumes that you will begin with Starting Tasks and have therefore included introductory information on all tasks within the Starting Tasks. A summary of the Advancing Task is provided after each Starting Task. This allows you to foresee what to expect as your Framework progresses. Each Advancing Task is then explained in detail within Sections 2.9, 2.10, 2.11 and 2.12.

Make sure that you keep good notes of what you do and how you do it. This will help you to repeat a task if you add to your Framework as well as help you transition to the Advancing Task.

2.3.4 Critical Starting Point
Whatever your organisation decides with regards to sections 2.3.1 to 2.3.3, the critical starting point for any development of your Framework is to be clear about where your organisation is, what its existing commitments are, what is already in place and what your organisation wants to achieve. This includes understanding your organisational culture and how things are done and get done. Without this, you may waste your time developing processes that are not in line with your organisational culture, remembering the culture onboard and onshore may be different.

2.4 Starting: Scoping And Planning
The first of the four areas will help you to identify where your organisation is currently, where your organisation would like to be and to collect information on your organisation's approach to managing regulatory requirements.

A good understanding of your organisation and where you want to progress to will enable you to affirm why you want to build your Framework and how you will do it.

2.4.1 Critical Starting Point: Understanding Your Organisation And The Bigger Picture
To get started, you initially need to examine these two fundamental questions:

- Where does my organisation stand now?
- Where does my organisation want to be in the future?

In order to tackle these overarching questions, we provide some example questions on the following two pages.

Answering these questions should not take long and there is no need to go into extensive detail. Simply look at what might be relevant for your organisation and its environmental and efficiency issues.

Understanding What Your Organisation Does

Start by considering the basic elements of your organisation and operations – in other words, 'what your organisation does'.

Depending on your organisation's role within the maritime industry, you should consider, for example, the following questions. Keep in mind that although you are able to influence the answer to the questions below, your organisation may not necessarily have the responsibility for the questions:

Ship Owner:
- How many ships do you own? What is their flag State, age, type and classification society? Who are your charterers and what are their charter terms? Do you operate and manage your ships?

Ship Operator:
- How many ships do you operate? What is their flag State, age, type and classification society? Who are your charterers (if it is not you) and what are their charter terms? Who are the owners? Who are your clients?

Ship Manager:
- How many ships do you manage? What is their flag State, age, type and classification society? Who are your charterers (if it is not you) and what are their charter terms? Who are the owners? Who are the operators? Who is in charge of the daily operation? Do you cooperate with all parties involved?

Charterer:
- How many ships do you charter? What is their flag State, age, type and classification society? Who are the owners and what are the charter terms? Do you operate and manage your chartered ships or if not, who does? Who is in charge of the daily operation? Do you cooperate with all parties involved?

These may appear to be obvious questions, but they will provide fundamental information about your organisation and therefore form the backbone of your Framework.

For example, if you solely charter out your ships, different activities and processes will be relevant compared to if you operate your own ships. Similarly, an approach might not make business sense if you only have two ships but may be highly relevant if you have a fleet of twenty ships. Some further questions that should be explored in order to ascertain 'what your organisation does' are provided below:

- Where do your ships voyage to? What principal States and ports do they visit? Are your operations primarily concerned with short sea shipping, inland waterways or international shipping?
- Do any of your ships have any environmental notations from classification societies? If so, which one and what does it cover?
- What are your organisation's strategic business objectives and how (if at all) do they link to your Framework?
- Who is responsible for the management of the International Management Code for the Safe Operation of Ships and for Pollution Prevention (ISM Code)?
- Who is responsible for ensuring compliance with regulatory requirements?
- What other management system, if any, do you have?
- If applicable: What port State detentions, flag State non-compliances, non-adherence to classification society's rules and/or rating agency downgrades have you had in the last three years? What were the reasons for them? What actions did your organisation take to address the findings and avoid recurrence of such situations?
- If applicable: What compliments or positive feedback have you received from port and flag States, classification societies and/or rating agencies in the last three years? What were the reasons for them? What did your organisation learn from them?

Again, these questions will enable you to start thinking about the specific circumstances of your organisation.

Your Organisation's Culture

Your organisation will have a specific culture, that is the unwritten approach to how things are done, who has influence, what is perceived as being right and wrong, and so on. This may well be different from what has been written down. Your organisation's culture may not be the same as that of your subcontractors, so for example the culture in a repair yard may be different.

It is necessary for you to be aware of what your organisational culture means in terms of how things get done, who decides, how public commitments are managed, etc. Keep a short description of your organisation's culture to help guide the development of your Framework. Keep it simple - it is not intended for inclusion in your Framework.

Understanding The Bigger Picture

The next action is to gain an understanding around how your organisation fits into the bigger picture of the maritime industry.

This can be facilitated by considering the example questions provided below:

- What client contract demands (if any) exist in relation to your environmental and efficiency issues?
- Who are your main competitors? What is their position on environmental and efficiency issues? Which actions, if any, have they taken to improve their environmental and efficiency issues?
- Which trade associations and/or organisations are you member of? What is their position on environmental and efficiency issues?
- Do you pay for fuel and if so always or only sometimes and why the difference (charter parties)?
- Who is responsible for crewing? Who is responsible for crew training? Are the people responsible the same for officers as for ratings?

The information gathered through asking these questions should give you an understanding of your organisation's operations and where your organisation sits in comparison to others. It should also help you to identify any patterns that may emerge with regard to environmental and efficiency issues.

Scoping & Planning
STARTING

2.4.2 Regulatory Requirements – Existing Processes

Regulations are in a constant state of change. New regulations are being developed and existing ones are constantly being modified and adapted.

It is therefore crucial to collect information on your organisation's approach to managing regulatory requirements and to establish what regulatory requirements your organisation has to comply with and how your organisation stays informed about any potential regulatory developments that could affect it. This does not only refer to regulatory developments at the International Maritime Organization (IMO), but also at a regional, port and flag State level, as applicable to your organisation's operations and its responsibilities with regards to regulatory compliance.

Your organisation will already have processes in place for identifying applicable regulatory requirements and ensuring compliance. This task is about identifying these processes and the regulatory requirements your organisation has already identified as applicable.

Familiarise yourself with the processes that your organisation uses to manage the identification of regulatory requirements and compliance and take notes regarding:

- What regulatory requirements does your organisation have to comply with?
- How does your organisation ensure regulatory compliance?
- Does this include solely IMO/flag or also relevant coastal/port State regulations?
- How does your organisation deal with regulatory requirements that apply to the ship but that your organisation is not responsible for? Who is responsible for possible non-compliance? Even if your organisation is not formally responsible for possible non-compliances, could it be held responsible by the media or the general public?

- What regulatory approaches of port States are of concern, such as the US Environmental Compliance Plan (ECP)?
- Is your organisation listed on a stock exchange? If so, are there any requirements you need to be aware of? For example, the United Kingdom requires organisations listed on the London Stock Exchange to report their greenhouse gas emissions.

There is an abundance of information and support available in the maritime industry regarding regulatory requirements and developments. The BIMCO website is one such source, as well as your classification society amongst others.

Part Two of the Guide to Maritime Environmental & Efficiency Management provides vital guidance, information and supplementary resources for all principal international and regional regulatory requirements that relate to environmental and efficiency issues.

Note down what you find with regards to the regulatory requirements that apply to your organisation and the processes you currently use to manage identification of regulatory requirements and compliance. Also note down what environmental aspects the regulations cover – this information will be used later in Task 2.4.5 and in Task 2.9.4.

The topic of regulatory requirements will be further explored in Task 2.9.2.

> **ADVANCING TASK**
> Include in your Framework the processes to consistently identify and update regulatory requirements and manage compliance.
> Please refer to Task 2.9.2 for further details.

2.4.3   Intention For Developing Your Framework

To help guide the development of your Framework, it is useful to be clear on why your organisation is developing it.

Additionally it would be useful to decide the approach to the development – refer back to Section 2.3.2 for some considerations.

To start this task, write down the intention for developing your Framework and the approach to its development. Then check that:

- It fits with your organisation's reality and culture.
- There are sufficient resources to achieve the intention.
- The intention is likely to be approved and supported.
- It fits with the guiding principles outlined in Section 2.2.
- It is supported by your organisation's strategic business objectives.

Please keep in mind that the intention may change due to circumstances and learning lessons along the way.

Get agreement for the intention before you proceed.

Scoping & Planning
STARTING

Determining Which Activities Your Framework Should Encompass

One of the critical tasks in developing your Framework is to determine which activities to include and when to include them. Consider whether you want to start building your Framework including all your organisation's activities or just some and if so, which ones.

In the context of your Framework, 'activity' is a broad term used for a set of processes that are needed to manage a specific undertaking, for example:

- Chartering.
- Crewing.
- Bunkering.
- Maintenance.

For example, the activity of bunkering would include, amongst others, the process of determining the empty tank volume, of ordering bunker fuel, of receiving it including noting it down in the Oil Record Book, paying for it, etc.

At this point you will need to draw information from the following points:

- What your organisation does.
- How your organisation fits into the bigger picture.
- The intention of the development of your Framework.

List all the activities that your organisation currently undertakes. Based on the list, suggest which initial activity (or activities) you want your Framework to cover. It may make sense to only include one activity at this point and extend the scope later on. You might find it useful to consult others on their opinion and gain agreement to proceed initially with that activity or those activities. Write down the initial activity/ activities your Framework will cover and if you have agreed on which activities are to be included next.

> **ADVANCING TASK**
> Include all the activities in your Framework.
> Please refer to Task 2.9.1 for further details.

Identifying The Environmental Aspects And Impacts Of Your Activity

The next task in continuing to build your Framework is to understand the environmental aspects associated with the activity you have included in your initial Framework and their impact on the environment.

What do we mean by environmental aspects and their impact on the environment?

'Aspects' are the environmental characteristics of a specific activity and 'Impact' is the effect this characteristic can have on the environment.

For example, if your activities include bunkering, one environmental aspect is the possibility of oil spills during bunkering. The impact would be the damage caused to the ocean and marine life by the oil spill.

In order to identify and understand the environmental aspects and impacts of the activity included in your initial Framework, look at the regulatory requirements applicable to your organisation. Environmental regulations not only set out the regulatory requirements, but also provide information on environmental aspects controlled by these requirements.

Understanding the environmental aspects and impacts of your activity does not mean that you need (or should) address them all in your Framework – especially not at this point. You may already have processes in place to manage these aspects, so if you wish, you can include these processes in your Framework later on.

At this stage, it is not important to determine the importance or significance of the environmental aspect of your activity, rather identify what they are and what they could be. Keep a list of your activity's environmental aspects and their impacts. Keep a note of how you carried out this task as you will come back to this when you add more activities to your Framework.

Further information on environmental aspects is included in Part Two of The Guide to Maritime Environmental & Efficiency Management.

> **ADVANCING TASK**
> Ensure all environmental aspects have been identified and then determine which are significant.
> Please refer to Task 2.9.4 for further details.

2.4.6 Identifying Risks

Scoping & Planning
STARTING

Risk is a term that is used almost on a daily basis, but it can have very different meanings, for example you may think of 'risk' as being 'the risk of':

- Your manager not agreeing to a pay rise.
- Being late for a meeting.
- Missing a train.
- Being made redundant.
- Suffering an accident.
- Dying.

For each of these cases, the probability of the risk happening and consequence if it happened vary significantly.

This task is not about discussing all of the risks related to your Framework, nor is it intended to provoke a detailed discussion about risks.

'Risk' in relation to your Framework relates to three elements:

1. Risk that environmental or efficiency issues will negatively impact your organisation's strategic business objectives *(NOTE: These are not the same as your Framework objectives, as covered in Task 2.10.2)*.
2. Risk that your organisation's strategic business objectives will negatively affect environmental or efficiency issues covered by your Framework.
3. Risk that your organisation will fail to meet your Framework's commitments and objectives, and for example become subject to port State regulatory approaches, such as US Coast Guard ECP.

In this task, we relate risk to the activity/activities you have decided to include initially in your Framework (Task 2.4.4), the intention for developing it (Task 2.4.3) as well as your organisation's strategic business objectives as far as they affect environmental and efficiency issues. We look at risk using a qualitative judgement.

Use the understanding of:

- What and who your organisation is including its culture which will have an embedded level of risk aversion specific to your organisation;
- your organisation's strategic business objectives;
- regulatory requirements and how they link to the activity/activities included in your Framework; and
- environmental aspects and their impacts on the environment and how they link to the specific activity you have chosen to include in your Framework.

Briefly identify the risks taking into account your organisation's strategic business objectives related to:

- Activity in your initial Framework;
- environmental aspects and impacts associated with that activity; and
- intention for developing your Framework.

This should just be a quick exercise, so please avoid going into too much detail at this stage. The main intention is for you to gain an overview of critical risks.

Examples of risks could be:

- An experienced employee leaving the organisation, resulting in you losing critical capacity to manage the environmental and efficiency issues of the activity in your Framework.
- Staff turnover which could result in processes related to the activity included in your Framework not being handed over adequately.
- Gaps in your understanding of regulatory requirements.
- Environmental aspects of the activity not being managed adequately.
- Changes in client demands related to the specific activity.
- Your organisation's strategic business objectives not allowing sufficient resources to undertake the development of your Framework as planned.

Having identified the risks, decide which risks impact 'critically' or 'less critically' on your organisation.

For example, the loss of an employee with significant experience of matters related to regulatory compliance would probably pose a critical risk. The regular loss of oil during bunkering would probably be a significant concern, whereas a rare loss of oil during bunkering probably would not be.

For those risks that you have rated as critical, think about what process can be put in place to lessen the potential impact of the risk.

As you develop your Framework further and include new activities, you will come back to this task to identify and evaluate risks related to these new activities.

ADVANCING TASK
Identifying and managing risks.
Please refer to Task 2.9.5 for further details.

2.5 Starting: Organising Your Approach

Once you have gained an initial understanding of where your organisation is and where you would like it to be, you can begin to organise how to get there.

This task principally entails organising the information that you have gathered and decisions that you have made in earlier tasks, framing them in such a way that they are understandable to others and anchoring them in your organisation's processes, systems, and culture.

2.5.1 Building A Mind Map Of Your Chosen Activities

STARTING

This task looks at creating a mind map of the activities you would like to include initially in your Framework and the different processes involved in these activities.

We advise you to first build a mind map for only one activity.

Building a mind map involves reviewing what the activities you identified in Task 2.4.4 are and which you agreed to include in your initial Framework. This should be done by a person with experience of the activity or process. We shall call this person a 'champion' from here on.

Ask your champion to identify:

- What processes are involved? For example, the activity of bunkering would include, amongst others, the process of determining the empty tank volume, of ordering bunker fuel, of receiving it including noting it down in the Oil Record Book, paying for it, etc.
- Do the environmental aspects identified in Task 2.4.5 relate to your activity's processes? If so, think about how you address these environmental aspects in your processes. Can you think of any other environmental aspects related to your activity's processes?
- Do the significant risks identified in Task 2.4.6 relate to your activity's processes? If so, think about how you address these risks in your processes. Can you think of any other risks related to your activity's processes?
- What existing approach does your organisation already have to manage the processes?
- What processes are not covered by an existing approach? Remember that the focus is on processes related to environment and efficiency.
- Who is going to be doing what to support the management of the processes?
- What competence do the people who are or will be involved in the processes need (skill, training etc.)?

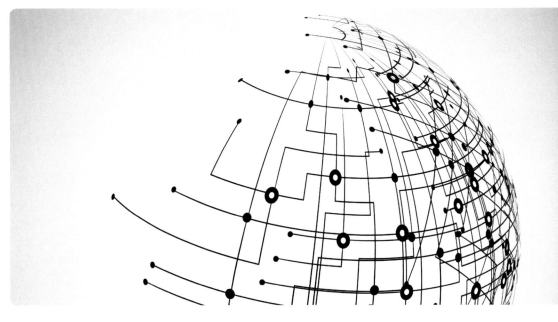

Please keep in mind that many processes will already be managed within your organisation, so try to adhere to established processes rather than developing new ones.

Please do not go beyond developing mind maps for the activities and their associated processes. This is because you need the insights from Tasks 2.5.2 and 2.5.3 before you can describe the activities and processes in more detail.

This mind mapping exercise can be repeated for any new activities that you add to your Framework.

ADVANCING TASK
Complete the mind maps of all activities.
Please refer to Task 2.10.3 for further details.

2.5.2

Learning From Existing Processes And Systems Within Your Organisation

To help you build your Framework, it is useful to learn from any existing systems that your organisation has built previously and is now operating. If your organisation has no existing systems, skip this task.

Additionally, it is likely that certain activities and related processes covered by your Framework are already managed by other systems within your organisation. To avoid overlap and to develop and operate your Framework as efficiently as possible, review these existing systems, see how they can be used to support your Framework and what is working well.

Ask the following questions related to your organisation's existing systems:

- What works well? Ask the people responsible and people using that system.
- What does not work? Ask the people responsible and people using that system.
- Do the existing systems cover some or all of the activities/processes included in your Framework?
- What sort of documented information does your organisation already use? Would they apply to your Framework?
- How do your existing systems set down what is done and what needs to be done?
- If applicable, how do you currently maintain the system for your ISM Code and how does that work? Could it be improved? Ask the people responsible and people using it.

Keep a note of the outcome of this evaluation so that you can use it to help you build your Framework.

2.5.3

Describing Activities And Processes Covered By Your Framework

In the early stages of developing your Framework, it is important to take a step back and think about how you would like to describe the activities and their associated processes included in your Framework.

Take a broad overview approach and think about how you would like to describe your Framework. Remember, there is not a right or wrong approach, only the one that works for your organisation and you.

Asking yourself the following question will assist you:

- How do you want your Framework to be described?
- What will need to be in writing and what could be documented more easily by means of pictures, images and/or diagrams? Remember to keep it simple.
- Would you like your activities to be described in paper or electronic format? What are the advantages and disadvantages of each option? Will it be the same for all activities?
- How do you agree on the content?
- How can you prevent changes to text, pictures etc. when they have been agreed on?
- How do you initiate and mange changes?
- How do you want to organise your documented information and where do you intend to store it?
- How do you want to keep the descriptions of activities and processes up-to-date? Try to come up with a simple and manageable way of doing this.

As your Framework develops, you will return to the questions above, so remember to keep notes of what you decide in relation to these questions.

2.5.4

Pulling It All Together

After having carried out the Tasks in 2.5.1, 2.5.2 and 2.5.3, it is now time to pull together the process descriptions from the activities included in your initial Framework.

For each process identified in Task 2.5.1, determine if you are using an existing process already or if you need to develop a new one.

With regard to existing processes, make a note of what they entail, who manages them and ensure that they cover the elements needed for your Framework.

Developing new processes requires expertise of the activity the process relates to. Therefore, this task is best executed by the champions identified in Task 2.5.1. Your task is to provide guidance to the champions and co-ordinate the development of new processes.

Based on the mind maps they have developed in Task 2.5.1, ask your champions to describe what the process should look like.

In describing the process, suggest that they:

- Start by using bullets, diagrams, pictures or flow charts (but not full text at this point) to describe the process. This way they can easily change things around and adjust the layout.
- Remind them to use something that works for your organisation. Please do not cut-and-paste from others unless it is written and communicated in your organisation's style and fits your organisation's operation.

If your Framework covers several activities, make sure that your selected champions communicate and exchange their ideas and thoughts on the processes they are describing. As your Framework's activities evolve, or you add activities, check that the processes are mutually consistent, that they link smoothly and that nothing is missing.

You will return to this when you add another activity to your Framework.

> **ADVANCING TASK**
> Pulling your Framework together.
> Please refer to Task 2.10.9 for further details.

Ensuring Competence

The smooth running of your Framework largely depends on the competence of the people developing it, applying it and using it. Therefore, competence is an important topic.

The 'champions' of the various processes (see Task 2.5.1) will have assumed a level of capability or competence to carry out a specific process.

At this point you should review the competence requirements for the different processes and see if anything strikes you as being excessively demanding, too easy or unreasonable in any other way. If this is the case, challenge the 'champions' of the process to explain the reasoning behind these requirements.

Competence will be re-visited in further detail in Task 2.10.4.

> **ADVANCING TASK**
> Ensuring competence and evaluating training needs.
> Please refer to Task 2.10.4 for further details.

Internal Communications

Communication is a vital element that will keep your Framework together and is unique to your organisational culture.

Communication exists on several levels:

- To individuals directly involved in the development of your Framework and activities included in it – both onshore and onboard.
- Building consciousness within the wider organisation.
- To external stakeholders.

This task deals with the first two levels, albeit at a basic level. More details are included in the corresponding Advancing Task.

Communicating With People Involved In The Development Of Your Framework

This internal communication task is specifically aimed at those individuals who are involved in the development of your Framework and the activities included in it.

At this stage, internal communication is about explaining to those individuals:

- What their responsibilities are, as envisaged at this early stage.
- How what they do relates to your Framework.
- What the relevant environmental aspects and impacts are.
- What the relevant critical risks are.

Raising Consciousness

Raising consciousness early on serves the purpose of gaining commitment and understanding from all, including individuals who may not be directly involved in the activities covered by your Framework. Aim to do this simply and consistently with your organisational culture.

Consciousness is about making sure people in your organisation are aware of:

- Why the organisation is developing your Framework.
- When it will be finished.
- What activities are covered within your Framework.

If your organisation is very small and you all work in the same place, raising consciousness and communicating with people involved in relevant activities may be accomplished in the natural course of day-to-day interactions. But for many organisations, making sure everyone stays in the loop, especially when you are not all in the same place, requires some effort.

Raising consciousness of and communicating with shore-based staff is relatively easy, but can be more complicated if reaching out to various ships and their crew. This is not only due to limited or insufficient communication channels such as the lack of internet and electronic modes of communication onboard, but also because of the variety of languages spoken by multinational crews.

ADVANCING TASK
Internal communications
Please refer to Task 2.10.5 for further details.

2.6 Starting: Safeguarding Your Progress

This area aims to determine how well your Framework is functioning and to ensure your organisation is on the right track to achieve the intentions for your Framework.

2.6.1 Collecting Information

Safeguarding Your Progress
STARTING

2.6.1
2.4.3 2.4.6

After your Framework has been in operation for some time, you can begin to gather information about what is working well and what is not. The way that you gather information and specifically how you communicate and report this information must take your organisational culture into account.

Because you have started small and your initial Framework does not include many activities, the level of information from your Framework will be limited. Nonetheless, it is important to evaluate the functioning of activities and processes included in your Framework.

For the processes and activities included in your Framework, ask yourself what information you will need to collect about processes/activities included in your Framework to determine:

- If your Framework is meeting its intention (see Task 2.4.3).
- If processes are functioning as required/specified.
- If critical risks (see Task 2.4.6) are managed appropriately.
- What needs to be changed to optimise your Framework.

Keep a note of the answers to the above questions as you will need them later for Task 2.11.1.

The next action within this task is to examine what information your organisation is already collecting, for what purpose and for whom. This will help you identify gaps between what information your organisation already has and what it still needs. This will also ensure you do not collect the same information twice, thus saving your organisation's resources and time.

Considering the information needs identified above and the information already collected, describe what information will still need to be collected to determine if your Framework meets its intention, if processes and risks are well managed, and if it functions as required.

In describing what information is required, set out to determine why it needs to be collected as well as how frequently, how to evaluate the information collected and what to do if the information indicates your Framework is not meeting its intentions or functioning as required.

Once you have compiled the list of information needs, challenge yourself by asking what information really is essential and what would simply be nice-to-have. Reduce this list to the essentials.

Remember to gain agreement from management regarding your proposed information collection process. As this is an iterative process, you can always come back, revise and adjust your process until you gain required agreements.

ADVANCING TASK
Identifying what you need to track.
Please refer to Task 2.11.1 for further details.

2.7
Starting: Staying On Track

This area focuses on reviewing your Framework, evaluating what needs to be improved and identifying and mitigating errors based on the activities included in the early development of your Framework.

2.7.1
Identifying And Mitigating Errors

Staying On Track

STARTING

When your Framework has been operating for some time you can begin to identify where your Framework is not functioning as required or where activities or processes are not carried out as described. This could be due to errors. At this point, the level of information from your Framework is limited because you will have started small, but for the processes included in your Framework it is beneficial to start considering how to identify errors and how to manage and correct them.

Errors can vary from being serious to less important.

Examples of errors may include:

- A planned process does not reflect practices onboard or onshore, it may be incorrectly described or difficult to follow as an example.
- Processes (correctly described) such as waste management are not adhered to.
- Failure to record data as required by a process.

Check how your organisation is currently dealing with errors. If there is already an established process, assess how you can adapt it to encompass the activities and processes included in your Framework.

If there is no established process in place, set out a simple process that includes descriptions for:

- What is considered an error in your Framework.
- How to minimise consequences of errors.
- What action to take to correct errors and how fast to take action.
- How to report errors, actions taken to correct them and to whom to report.
- How to evaluate errors to identify learning lessons.

Describe this process and incorporate it into your Framework.

ADVANCING TASK
Identifying near misses.
Please refer to Task 2.12.1 for further details.

2.8
Advancing Tasks

As described in Section 2.3.2, building your Framework involves tasks of varying complexity which is why tasks have been divided into Starting and Advancing Tasks.

Here we detail the Advancing Tasks. For each Advancing Task, we have noted if there is a linked Starting Task and where to find it, so you can easily refer back to it if necessary.

2.9 Advancing: Scoping And Planning

Here you will review the information from Area 2.4 ('Starting: Scoping and Planning') and add additional tasks related to regulatory compliance, availability of resources and promises made by the organisation.

2.9.1 Reviewing What Activities You Want Your Framework To Encompass
Linked to Starting Task 2.4.4

Scoping & Planning
ADVANCING

As your experience of building your Framework grows, review the activities included in your initial Framework, the approach taken to select activities and identify which activities are not yet included in your Framework.

To complete this task, review the list you developed in Section 2.4.4, see if your organisation is undertaking any new activities and identify which activities are not yet – but ideally should be - included in your Framework.

Write down which activities you want your Framework to cover and why, and add a short description of each activity. Before moving on, you need to gain management agreement to the proposed scope of your Framework.

Later tasks may add activities to your Framework. If this is the case, come back to this task and add these activities to the list.

2.9.2 Regulatory Requirements
Linked to Starting Task 2.4.2

Scoping & Planning
ADVANCING

This task involves including your organisation's existing processes for identifying regulatory requirements and management and evaluation of compliance into your Framework - if you have not already done so.

In Task 2.4.2, you have collected information on your organisation's approach to managing regulatory requirements, what regulatory requirements your organisation has to comply with and how your organisation stays informed about any potential regulatory developments that could affect it.

Building upon Task 2.4.2, this Advancing Task includes three actions:

1. Agreement on how far beyond current regulatory requirements you wish to scan the horizon to be forewarned about future regulatory requirements.
2. Confirming or adjusting the current processes used to identifying what regulatory requirements apply to your organisation.
3. Confirming or adjusting the current processes used to manage and evaluate compliance with regulatory requirements.

Scanning The Horizon
In terms of the first action, based on your organisation's strategic business objectives, ask and gain consensus on the question 'when should your organisation start to take account of regulatory requirements'. For example, will it be:

- Just before the regulation enters into force;
- For an existing Convention: when it is being amended;
- For a new Convention:
  - When it enters into force;
  - When it is adopted;
  - When it is drafted.

Keep notes of the agreement reached with regards to scanning the horizon.

Processes To Identify Applicable Regulatory Requirements

In terms of your current processes for identifying regulatory requirements and the regulatory requirements collected in Task 2.4.2, you now need to review them both for their consistency and fit with your Framework in relation to:

- Your organisation's strategic business objectives including what port State regulatory approaches are of concerns such as US Coast Guard ECP.
- The level of horizon scanning agreed above.
- The activities included in your Framework from Task 2.9.1, including the information from Task 2.4.1.
- The intention of your Framework from Task 2.4.3.

Make sure the process includes:

- Under which circumstances a regulatory requirement applies to your organisation – i.e. because your organisation has direct responsibility or because it applies through commercial contract.
- What horizon scanning agreement was reached, see above.
- How to ensure your organisation consistently identifies regulatory requirements that apply to it.
- How to evaluate regulatory requirements to identify what they require specifically of your organisation and which processes in your Framework need to be adjusted to take account of regulatory requirements and their changes.
- Whom to inform about changes in regulatory requirements and their consequences for processes in your Framework.
- How frequently regulatory requirements need to be reviewed.
- What competences are needed for the person identifying and updating regulatory requirements.
- What records need to be kept of the process.

As applicable to your evaluation, revise, update or use the existing processes and incorporate them into your Framework.

Processes To Manage And Evaluate Compliance

The final action of this Advancing Task is to ensure that your organisation's processes for managing and evaluating compliance are consistent with the previous two actions for the task above and meet the intention of your Framework.

Review your current processes for evaluating and managing regulatory compliance for their consistency and fit with your Framework in relation to:

- Your organisation's strategic business objectives including what port State regulatory approaches are of concerns such as US Coast Guard ECP.
- The outcome of the two actions above.
- The activities included in your Framework from Task 2.9.1 including the information from Task 2.4.1.
- The intention of your Framework from Task 2.4.3.

Make sure the process includes:

- How your organisation is going to ensure compliance for each regulatory requirement.
- Who is responsible for ensuring compliance with each regulatory requirement.
- Who is responsible for regularly evaluating and reporting on overall compliance.
- How to conduct the evaluation of overall compliance.
- Whom to tell about the outcome of the evaluation of overall compliance.
- What action to take should the evaluation indicate that your organisation is not in compliance.
- How frequently your organisation needs to review and repeat the task of evaluating compliance.
- What are the competence requirements for staff responsible for compliance, for evaluating compliance and for reporting on it.
- What records need to be kept.

As applicable to your evaluation, revise, update or use the existing processes and incorporate them into your Framework.

2.9.3 Understanding What Your Key Stakeholders Demand And Expect From You

No Link to Starting Task

This task considers demands that are placed on your organisation by its stakeholders, as relevant to your situation, such as:

- Clients.
- Shareholders.
- Employees.
- Ship owner associations.
- Ship yards.
- Classification societies (outside their role as Recognised Organisations).
- Banks.
- The World Business Council for Sustainable Development.
- Groups interested in shipping and environmental issues such as the Clean Cargo Working Group and WWF International as relevant to your situation.

First, you need to decide which stakeholders you wish to consider. It is likely that clients, shareholders (if you have any) and trade associations (if you are a member) are the minimum stakeholders to be included in your Framework. Please keep a list of the relevant stakeholders and why you chose them.

Next, consider what their demands are. Information on demands can be found in contracts, shareholder discussions/minutes of meetings as well as trade association commitments etc.

Below is a set of non-exhaustive questions that will help you identify and understand your stakeholders' demands:

- What are 'contract' requirements of your clients (charterers, owners etc.) in relation to environmental and efficiency issues?
- What are the (contractual) requirements of your outside agents (e.g. classification societies, trade associations, rating agents) in relation to environmental and efficiency issues?
- If applicable, what are your shareholders' requirements in relation to environmental and efficiency issues?
- What are the requirements of your other stakeholders (only those that you wish to consider) in relation to environmental and efficiency issues?
- Are there any other external or internal critical institutions (who you have not included in your stakeholders identified above) whose views in relation to environmental and efficiency issues you must take into account? If so, what are their views and demands?
- Within the next five years, how do you expect that your stakeholders' demands (as identified above) in relation to environmental and efficiency issues will change? What new demands do you expect them to have?

Having identified what stakeholder demands your organisation needs to fulfil, you now need to establish two processes:

1. How to identify and update stakeholder demands.
2. Check that you organisation is meeting these stakeholder demands.

Identifying And Updating Stakeholder Demands

In order to develop a process for identifying and updating stakeholder's demands, determine:

- How to decide which stakeholders to consider in the identification and evaluation of stakeholder demands.
- How to identify stakeholder demands your organisation needs to fulfil.
- How to evaluate stakeholder demands to identify what they require specifically of your organisation and which processes in your Framework need to be adjusted to take account of stakeholder demands.
- Whom to inform about changes in stakeholder demands and their consequences for processes in your Framework.
- How frequently stakeholder demands need to be reviewed.
- Which competences the person identifying and updating stakeholder demands needs.
- What records need to be kept of the process.

As you describe this process, reflect on what you have learnt from identifying stakeholder demands above and improve/amend the process accordingly.

Ensuring Stakeholder Demands Are Met
An important task for your organisation is to ensure that it meets stakeholder demands.

To ensure this is done consistently and at intervals suitable for your organisation, you need a process which sets out how your organisation will ensure it meets these demands.

Based on the identification and evaluation of stakeholder demands, this process will set out:

- How you are going to ensure your organisation meets each relevant stakeholder demand.
- Who is responsible for ensuring your organisation meets each relevant stakeholder demand.
- Who is responsible for regularly evaluating and reporting on how your organisation meets all its stakeholder demands.
- How to conduct the evaluation of how your organisation meets stakeholder demands.
- Who to tell about the outcome of this evaluation.
- What action to take should the evaluation indicate that your organisation is not meeting stakeholder demands.
- How frequently your organisation needs to review and repeat the task of evaluating if it meets stakeholder demands.
- What are the competence requirements for staff responsible for evaluating if your organisation is meeting stakeholder demands, and for reporting on it.
- What records need to be kept.

2.9.4

Determining The Significance Of Your Organisation's Environmental Aspects
Linked to Starting Task 2.4.5

In Starting Task 2.4.5, you examined the environmental aspects of your organisation's activities included in your initial Framework.

Advancing means two additional actions:

1. Completing the identification of environmental aspects and impacts associated with all activities included in your Framework.
2. Determining which aspects and impacts are significant to your organisation.

Initially review your actions from Task 2.4.5 plus the outcome of tasks carried out so far to determine if your list of environmental aspects and impacts is complete or needs adjusting based on activities added and learning lessons as you built your Framework.

The second action listed above involves establishing your significance criteria and then evaluating the revised list of environmental aspects to determine their significance. Your organisation will manage its environmental aspects (as it does its risks) via two approaches:

- Non-significant environmental aspects will be managed via processes in your Framework that ensure you meet regulatory requirements, stakeholder demands and collect information to show you meet such requirements and demands.
- Significant environmental aspects where, in addition to above processes, your organisation will make specific commitments, set specific objectives or have specific information gathering requirements.

You need to determine significance criteria specific to your organisation.

This involves a decision on what your organisation will deem as significant. In order to do this, the following questions may prove helpful:

- Are we going to make all environmental aspects that have a large impact on the environment significant? – And how do we determine what is a large impact on the environment?
- Are we going to make all environmental aspects related to regulatory requirements significant?
- Are we going to make all environmental aspects related to stakeholder demands significant?
- Are we going to make all environmental aspects that result in high safety risks significant?
- Are there any environmental aspects or impacts that your organisation focuses on for other reasons that should be significant?

Having evaluated your answers to the questions above and taking into account your organisation's strategic business objectives, develop significance criteria applicable to your organisation and ensure these criteria have been agreed on by relevant people. At this point keep it simple.

Based on your significance criteria, evaluate the list of all the environmental aspects to determine which of them are most important.

Identifying, Evaluating And Updating Your Environmental Aspects And Impacts - Process

Whilst it is relatively easy to identify your organisation's environmental aspects and impacts and determine their significance as a one-off action, it is important that this is repeated on a regular basis and in a consistent manner.

In order to develop a process that will allow you to keep the environmental aspects and associated impacts and their significance up-to-date, you need to decide:

- How to evaluate your organisation's activities, regulatory requirements and stakeholder demands to identify your organisation's environmental aspects and impacts.
- How to determine criteria for what makes an environmental aspect significant.
- How and when to update the process for determining significance criteria.
- How to evaluate environmental aspects to determine if they are significant or not.
- Who to tell about changes in your significant environmental aspects and impacts and their consequences for processes in your Framework.
- Who to tell about changes in your process for determining significance criteria and their consequences for processes in your Framework.
- How frequently your organisation needs to review its environmental aspects and impacts and their significance.
- Which competences the person conducting the evaluation of environmental aspects and impacts requires.
- What records need to be kept of the process.

As you describe this process, reflect on what you have learnt from identifying environmental aspects and their associated impacts, from determining significance criteria and applying them to environmental aspects. Amend and improve the process accordingly.

Identifying And Managing Risks
Linked to Starting Task 2.4.6

Task 2.4.6 outlined a basic method for identifying and assessing risks. This task, as a follow-on, builds on this method and aims to help you identify and evaluate your risks, determine which risks need mitigation and/or management and how to follow-up on them.

As a reminder, 'risk' in your Framework relates to three elements:

1. The risk that environmental or efficiency issues will negatively impact your organisation's strategic business objectives. (*NOTE: These are not the same as your Framework objectives, as covered in Task 2.10.2.*)
2. The risk that your organisation's strategic business objectives will negatively affect environmental or efficiency issues covered by your Framework.
3. The risk that you will fail to meet your Framework's commitments and objectives, including what port State regulatory approaches are of concern, such as the US ECP.

Identifying Risks

Relating to the three elements listed above and the activities covered in your Framework, use the following to identify a list of possible risks:

*   Who your organisation is, what it does and what the organisational culture is.
*   What your organisation's strategic business objectives are. (*NOTE: If your organisation is listed on the stock market, your Finance team will have a risk register for your organisation. It is useful to have a look at it and keep it in your mind.*)
*   Regulatory requirements and how they link to the activities in your Framework.
*   Stakeholder demands and how they link to the activities in your Framework.
*   Environmental aspects and their impacts on the environment and how they link to the activities in your Framework.
*   Significant environmental aspects and commitments made in connection with them.
*   Your organisation's approach to managing regulatory requirements and stakeholder demands.
*   If applicable, historical events where your organisation was unable to meet regulatory requirements or stakeholder demands and any inherent weakness which led to these incidents.
*   If applicable, records of accidents that caused harm to the environment.

Based on this information, identify the risks that relate to the activities covered in your Framework and which of the three elements they are linked to and note them down.

Evaluating Risks

The next action is to evaluate your risk. A good starting point is to discuss risks with a group of other people involved in the development of your Framework.

Within the group, develop and agree a common understanding of the meaning of high, medium and low risks for your organisation taking into account your organisation's strategic business objectives and culture of risk aversion and write this down.

Based on this understanding, evaluate all the risks identified and rank them as high, medium or low. Review your evaluation of risks critically and check if there are any inconsistencies in grading risks. If anything seems illogical, review your decision.

The most important risk areas for your organisation will probably be:

- Those associated with regulatory requirements that would impact your ability to operate.
- Any demands from stakeholders that would impact your ability to operate.
- Those affecting your strategic business objectives.

Even though not every risk has an immediate financial consequence, it can still have negative financial consequences in the long run, such as causing harm to the brand and reputation of your organisation. Avoiding such harm and protecting your good brand name and reputation can be critical in convincing charterers/owners/clients and regulators that you are reliable. This will help you secure business and protect your organisation.

Mitigating, Managing And Following Up On Risks

For each risk that the group has graded as high, you need to decide if you can mitigate the impact of its occurrence and if so, how and which actions your organisation could take.

For high risks that cannot be mitigated, you need to devise a plan for how your organisation would manage and respond if the risk materialised.

You may also choose to keep an eye on some of the medium risks to make sure you can adjust mitigation response accordingly should the risk suddenly become high. This will help mitigate the impact of high risks in the future.

NOTE: A risk's grading can change over time going either up or down.

Based on the tasks above and the decisions you have taken, compile a list setting out:

- Risks and the result of the evaluation.
- Risks to be mitigated and how.
- Risks to be managed and how.

Process For Identifying And Managing Risks

In order to make it easier for you (and/or other people) to repeat this task in the future, describe the process related to identifying, evaluating and managing risks. More specifically, describe:

- How to identity risks.
- How to evaluate risk; and the criteria for grading risks as high, medium or low.
- How to deal with high risks and how to determine mitigation actions or management approaches.
- How to assess the effectiveness of your organisation's risk mitigation actions and management approaches.
- How to deal with medium risks and how to determine which risks your organisation should keep an eye on.
- Whom to tell about changes in your high risks and their consequences for processes in your Framework.
- How frequently to review existing risks and identify and evaluate potential new ones.
- How frequently to check and assess mitigation and management actions for high risks.
- Who is responsible for identifying, evaluating and managing risks and which competences is this person required to have to execute this task.
- What records need to be kept related to this task.

Describing this process is also a good opportunity to reflect on what you have learnt from identifying and evaluating risks and how you can use this experience to improve and amend the process.

Commitments
No Link to Starting Task

Commitments are pledges made by senior management on what they want to achieve related to the activities included in your Framework.

For example, an organisation could commit to meet regulatory requirements when they are adopted.

Developing And Agreeing Commitments

You can facilitate the process of gaining commitment from senior management by drafting and suggesting commitments that are both realistic and that align with your organisation's wider strategic business objectives.

In order to tackle this, try to find out:

- What commitments your organisation has already made that apply to the activities within your Framework.
- What your organisation's financial health is and hence what commitments could it afford in terms of resources.
- What senior management's general view is in terms of environmental and efficiency issues.
- What level of support you could realistically get.
- What your organisational culture is and how it affects the way you agree on and communicate commitments.

Take the information that you find from the above points, together with a review of the activities covered by your Framework (Task 2.9.1), regulatory requirements (Task 2.9.2), stakeholder demands (Task 2.9.3), significant environmental aspects (Task 2.9.4), high risks (Task 2.9.5) and draft a set of commitments that your organisation could make.

The next action is to ask yourself for which of the draft commitments you could realistically get support and funding.

Before approaching senior management to gain agreement, think about how to 'sell' the proposed commitments including information on links with strategic business objectives and available resources. Also identify who the actual decision-makers are and who is influencing them in the background. These two groups need to be convinced first.

As part of Task 2.12.3, your organisation should be regularly reviewing its commitments.

2.10 Advancing: Organising Your Approach

This area deals with completing the tasks related to mapping your activities, competence, communication, raising consciousness of your Framework.

2.10.1 Your Framework Policy

No Link to Starting Task

This task focuses on your organisation's Framework policy. It outlines the commitments your organisation makes related to the activities covered by your Framework and provides some other basic information about your organisation.

For this task, you need to review your organisation's commitments (Task 2.9.6), what your organisation does and how it fits into the larger picture (Task 2.4.1).

While your Framework policy will differ from other organisations, policies typically include information such as:

*   Who your organisation is, what it does and what the organisational culture is.
*   What activities and processes your Framework covers.
*   What commitments your organisation has made and who has agreed to these commitments.
*   When the policy will be reviewed.

Develop your Framework policy making sure it is relevant to your organisation and achievable. Discuss it with relevant people, revise it if necessary and get management sign-off for the policy. Another important point you and senior management need to agree on is whether or not the Framework policy will be available to stakeholders and other parties.

NOTE: The policy is not just a 'piece of paper on a wall' but should be the guiding tool for your organisation to ensure all employees and others fulfil the organisation's aims and commitments. It may well form part of evaluating individuals' performance.

As part of Task 2.12.3, your organisation should be regularly reviewing its Framework policy.

2.10.2 Objectives

This task is about setting objectives for your Framework. Objectives arise from commitments your organisation makes, as well as significant environmental aspects and high risks. An objective sets out how your organisation plans to achieve commitments and often also by when.

For example, if your organisation's commitment was to meet regulatory requirements when they are adopted, your objective could be to initiate process changes necessary to deliver these 6 months before adoption.

In order to determine your objectives, review the information you have collected to date and your evaluation in relation to:

- What you do and what your organisational culture is.
- How your organisation fits into the bigger picture.
- Activities covered by your Framework.
- Regulatory requirements.
- Stakeholder demands.
- Significant environmental aspects and impacts.
- High risks and their mitigation and management.
- Commitments and policy statement.

Based on this information, draft your objectives. These can be short, medium or long-term such as the next 18 months and 5 years.

Your objectives need to be approved by management and acceptable to the organisation, so test your objectives by asking:

- Do they fit the organisation's culture and aims?
- Are they consistent with the commitments and policy?
- Does the organisation have enough resources to deliver on them?
- Are they consistent with the activities included in your Framework?
- Are any of them only nice-to-haves that could wait?

Revise your draft objectives in light of the above.

Consult on your draft objectives and explain the outcome of the test above to show you have taken account of what is feasible for your organisation. The representatives that you might consult with typically include:

- Senior management.
- Representatives who manage resources you would need to deliver the objectives.
- Representatives who would have to contribute significantly to achieve your objectives.
- Representatives with responsibility for regulatory compliance and for managing your ISM Code (if applicable).

Adjust the objectives in light of comments and finalise them for your Framework. You might need project plans to deliver on your objectives.

As part of Task 2.12.3, your organisation should regularly review its objectives.

2.10.3 Building A Comprehensive Map Of Activities And Processes
Linked to Starting Task 2.5.1

In the Starting Task 2.5.1, your champions drew up mind maps of the initial activities covered in your Framework. You may even already have repeated this task to cover new activities.

Refer back to the activities set out in Task 2.9.1 and:

* Identify for which activities you still need to develop mind maps.
* Using the relevant champions, develop mind maps for these activities and their processes.
* Consult people involved in the different activities and processes to see if the mind maps are complete and ensure what your champions think is being done is what is actually being done.
* Ask the champions to re-adjust their mind maps in light of consultation.

Check the mind maps to see if there any overlaps in processes and if so, if these could be organised more efficiently. This is also a good opportunity to check for excess bureaucracy and identify how to minimise it.

2.10.4 Ensuring Competence And Identifying Training Needs
Linked to Starting Task 2.5.5

Your organisation's staff and crew are key to successful implementation of your Framework. It is therefore important to ensure that everyone involved in your Framework is appropriately competent.

Competence is based on four key elements:

* Practical and theoretical knowledge.
* Skills.
* Abilities.
* Personal attributes.

Depending on the process, not each element is required equally. It is therefore important to determine what kind of knowledge, skills, abilities and personal attributes are required for each activity and associated processes. You will need to seek your champions' help to determine this.

Ensuring competence and identifying training needs involves three actions:

1. Establishing a common process for determining and evaluating competence.
2. Determining competence criteria for activities and associated processes within your Framework.
3. Evaluating individuals' competence for a specific activity or process, determining what competencies are missing and identifying ways to fill any gaps.

With all these actions, keep in mind that the focus is on activities covered by your Framework and on processes resulting from other tasks involved in developing your Framework.

Also recognise and accept that you cannot determine competence criteria and evaluate a person's competence by yourself. You will need to rely on your 'champions' and their expertise of a specific activity.

This approach is iterative and the critical focus is to keep it simple and challenge anything that looks too complex.

Process For Determining Competence Criteria And Evaluating Competence

This outline process will be used to define competence criteria for activities and their associated processes within your Framework.

This is an iterative task, so expect to have to change the process as it is used.

Typically a competence determination and evaluation process covers:

- How to determine the competence criteria for a specific activity.
- How to determine which competence criteria are critical for a specific task.
- How to evaluate someone's competence related to a specific activity.
- How to bridge any gaps identified during the evaluation of an individual's competence.
- How frequently to determine which competence criteria are needed for an activity.
- What information is needed in order to evaluate an individual's competence.
- What competences the individuals who determine and evaluate competence require.

The two actions below will provide you with valuable feedback on this process. This will allow you to adjust the determination and evaluation of competence.

Determining Competence Criteria For Activities Within Your Framework

Your next action within this task is to ask your champions to determine the applicable competence criteria based on the above process. Remember to suggest they should look at what competence criteria already exist for the activity as duplication is not helpful.

Make sure that the competence criteria you get back from the champions are:

- **Reasonable** – If the criteria are more demanding than they realistically need to be, this will increase costs for your organisation. If they are too low, the risk of failing the process is high.
- **Consistent** – Similar processes should require similar competences.
- **Achievable** – Several people within the organisation are likely to meet the competence requirements.

Ask each champion to describe the competence criteria for the activity they are dealing with, using a common layout to help you integrate these into the various activity/process descriptions.

Ensure competence criteria are updated regularly based on changes and learning lessons.

Evaluating Individuals' Competence For A Specific Activity Within Your Framework And Identifying Gaps

With the competence criteria for each applicable activity/process and the process from Action 1 ('Establishing a common process for determining and evaluating competence'), you can now start evaluating people currently performing the activity/process or identified as due to perform the activity/process.

The actual evaluation should be performed by the manager of the person based on the competence criteria relevant for the activity and developed in Action 2 ('Determining competence criteria for activities and associated processes within your Framework').

Ask the manager to make a note of any gaps, if they are critical and if so how to deal with gaps. Additionally, ask for feedback on the competence criteria identified for the specific activity.

If training needs are identified, remember that a lot of training can be 'on the job'. Other training will be available outside your organisation. To make sure training is effective, evaluate the training and its results.

When providing training, keep in mind that new skills and behaviours may be abandoned if not practised and supported and old habits may become the norm again. Continuous support and possibilities to take training again can counteract this risk.

Complete this action ensuring it covers all the activities in your Framework.

Evaluate the fit between the competence criteria for an activity and that displayed by the process holder(s) on a regular basis.

2.10.5

Internal Communications
Linked to Starting Task 2.5.6

Organising Your Approach
ADVANCING

Starting Task 2.5.6 outlined the approach to communicating with individuals involved in the development of your Framework as well as raising consciousness across your organisation – both at a basic level.

In this task, we are still dealing with these two actions, but in greater detail and related to more activities.

Communicating With Individuals Involved In The Development Of Your Framework

As part of the Starting Task 2.5.6, you will have already told individuals involved in the development of your Framework:

- What their responsibilities are.
- How what they do relates to your Framework.
- What the relevant environmental aspects and impacts are.
- What the relevant critical risks are.

Now, you can also update them on:

- What the policy commitments and objectives are.
- How your Framework functions.

In addition, all individuals involved in your Framework need to know more about their specific tasks and responsibilities. In relation to their task, provide detail related to the regulatory requirements, environmental effects, risks, stakeholder demands, emergency preparedness and suggestions on what to do if things do not go according to plan.

Remember to communicate this information in line with your organisational culture as that will affect how well your message is received and understood.

Furthermore, explain:

- How their specific task fits into and impacts on the success of your Framework.
- How it relates to other tasks and other people's responsibilities.
- How to deal with any overlaps of tasks.

Please consider that communicating to ship-based staff is somewhat more complicated than to onshore staff. This may be due to insufficient communication channels such as the lack of internet and electronic modes of communication onboard, but also because of the variety of languages spoken by multinational crews. It is also much easier to communicate face-to-face which is often not possible with an individual with responsibility for communicating with the crew on a specific ship.

Careful thought therefore needs to be given to how and at what stage the crew are communicated to.

Raising Consciousness Across Your Organisation

Informing all staff (and as necessary contractors) about your organisation's Framework, its content and functioning as well as the reasoning behind it is imperative.

It will help getting commitment and support for your Framework within the whole organisation and help to ensure that individuals' actions do not compromise it. Ideally, the entire organisation will make a joint effort to realise your organisation's Framework commitments.

More specifically, provide information to them on:

- The reasons for developing your Framework and its importance to the organisation.
- The commitments and objectives of your Framework.
- The activities covered by your Framework.
- How they interact with your Framework.
- Who is responsible for the operation of your Framework - this may be more than one person.

Identify different ways to make all staff (and as necessary contractors) aware of your Framework. To get this information out efficiently, you can look for opportunities through existing business meetings and events or other existing communication channels, e.g. presentation at annual meetings or an update in the organisation newsletter. Think about how frequently you want to raise consciousness about your Framework within the wider organisation.

The process of raising consciousness with the crew and officers onboard presents additional challenges in terms of planning and delivering information. There are obvious issues to take account of such as distances, variation in time zones, numerous languages, regular changes in crew due to rest times of the ship, limited interfaces between members onboard and the hierarchical structure and culture onboard, which will be different from that onshore.

Furthermore, it is worth remembering that the crew does not have 24 hour internet access, nor do they commonly have laptops/desktops for use at work. Additional challenges include the possible interface between you and the crew due to use of managing agents and management companies.

Therefore, you may need to consider talking to the crew when they are in port, gathering them together at some point, remembering to regularly refresh the messages as crew changes, tailoring your message to the relevant crew speciality, making sure they understand what they can do to improve and support your Framework.

Also consider what languages are spoken across your organisation and consider if you need to make information about your Framework available in some of these languages.

Raising consciousness also serves the purpose of gaining employees' agreement to support your Framework. Be prepared to encounter resistance. You can reduce this resistance by actively including employees in the development of your Framework by asking for ideas, feedback, etc. This will also improve the quality of your Framework as each employee has very specific knowledge and is an expert in its specific field. Actively asking for this expertise will therefore make your Framework more useful and more aligned to your organisation's reality and practices.

Describe a process that covers:

- What, when and how often to tell employees.
- What, when and how often to tell contractors.
- Whose support to ask for raising consciousness in the wider organisation.
- How often to review and update this process.

2.10.6 Communicating Externally
No Link to Starting Task

As your Framework comes together, you may wish to communicate your organisation's environmental and efficiency developments and achievements to your stakeholders – as defined in Task 2.9.3. This is a very 'personal' decision specific to your organisational culture.

However, please remember that there is no requirement to do so. The decision as to whether or not to tell stakeholders about your Framework and its achievements is entirely up to you and your organisation.

Nonetheless, there are likely to be benefits in communicating successful environmental initiatives as stakeholder consciousness of environmental issues grows. Furthermore, you may have commitments that come with memberships and standards you decided to comply with – these may require you to provide information on your environmental behaviour.

If you decide to communicate to your stakeholders, you should develop a process for how to do it. Please consult your PR and legal teams when doing so.

Together, you can decide:

- What you want to tell stakeholders and in how much detail; and
- what message you want to convey.

Typical information to include when communicating externally may be:

- The company commitment and policy.
- Why you are doing this.
- What your objectives are.
- What the benefits are.
- Examples of positive developments and achievements.

2.10.7 Responding To Stakeholder Questions
No Link to Starting Task

This task is about reacting to requests, whether from those stakeholders you have identified in Task 2.9.3 or others.

The previous task was about your choice to communicate proactively with stakeholders and your choice as to which stakeholders you wished to communicate with. However, this task addresses situations where you have no choice about who communicates with you, but you can decide about how you want to respond.

Establish what your organisation already does when it receives a query, question or complaint. It is likely that your organisation already has a process in place for how to deal with these. If this is the case, think of possibilities of how to adopt and amend that process to fit your Framework.

2.10.8 Emergency Preparedness
No Link to Starting Task

In order to prepare for emergencies, it is essential that you consider:

- Which environmental aspects may result in an emergency situation?
- Which risks may result in an emergency situation?
- Which activities in your Framework may result in an emergency situation?
- What lessons have been learned from previous errors?

Define what constitutes an emergency for your organisation, how you need to react to it and how to reduce the impacts of an emergency. Include in your process description how to identify learning lessons from an emergency.

If your organisation has an ISM Code management system, it will already have a process related to emergency preparedness and management. This makes a great starting point for this task.

Remember to set out a process on how to review this task, the competences of people having to deal with an emergency, whom to report to, etc.

2.10.9 Pulling Your Framework Together
Linked to Starting Task 2.5.4

This task is mainly a reminder to check that you have collated all the process descriptions from the various activities and processes included in your Framework.

If you have not got a complete set of descriptions, go back to Task 2.5.4 and conduct the task outlined in it for all the activities and processes that are now included in your Framework.

In pulling together your Framework, ensure that all the process descriptions that have been developed are consistent and make sense in your organisation's specific circumstances.

2.11 Advancing: Safeguarding Your Progress

This area looks at what you can do to safeguard that your Framework is taking your organisation where it wants to be and how you can check that matters are going according to the plan set out within your Framework.

2.11.1 Identifying What You Need To Track

Linked to Starting Task 2.6.1

Safeguarding Your Progress
ADVANCING

It is important to collate all relevant information that will show how your Framework is functioning to all the relevant people in your organisation.

This will give them the assurance that your Framework is delivering on its commitments. This information will also help to provide an incentive to improve your Framework, its overall functioning and help to celebrate success.

The task is to find out what information is needed to evaluate that your Framework is:

- Consistently functioning as defined in its processes.
- Delivering on its commitments and objectives.
- Capable of flagging failures to address changes in regulatory requirements, environmental aspects and impacts, and risks at a stage where such failure can be addressed.

To identify the relevant information, you need to understand the following:

- What information management needs to be assured of your Framework delivering – this may be different from your expectation.
- What information staff involved in your Framework need to be assured of your Framework delivering – this may be different from you expectation and different from management needs.
- What information your stakeholders (those you have decided in Task 2.9.3) need to be assured of your Framework delivering – again, this may be different from your expectation, that of management and that of people involved in your Framework.
- What information your organisation needs to flag if regulatory requirements, risks, environmental aspects and impacts change and no action is taken to address those changes.
- What information your organisation needs to draw attention to changes in regulatory compliance status.
- What information your organisation needs to flag failure to meet stakeholder demands.
- What information your organisation needs to learn from errors.

In looking at what information to collect, you need to be aware of how your organisation already collects information, what it collects and how it establishes how it meets commitments, plans, budgets etc.

Having evaluated the answers to the above bullet points, plus incorporating the approaches your organisation has in place, you can now propose what information needs to be collected and how frequently. Test your proposal out with relevant staff.

To be effective and consistent, the information gathering process should be repeatable. In order to ensure this, you need a process to describe how this is done.

The following questions will help to develop and describe this process:

- What frequency of information collection is needed to meet the certainty expected?
- Where do you get your information from (data sources)?
- How frequently do you need to collect information?
- Who is/will be responsible for the various phases in the collection of information and for what information?
- Who is responsible for analysing or evaluating the information?
- What needs to be done if information is missing?
- What needs to be done if the information indicates that here is an issue?
- What needs to be done when information shows your Framework is failing to deliver on its commitments? Some commitments may be more critical than others.
- How can you share information and ensure it is safe?
- What information needs to be reported, how and to whom?

You can now describe a process to collect and manage information that works for your organisation and that ensures the repeatability and consistent application of the process. This should include an element of reviewing what information to gather to meet the needs of your Framework.

This is an iterative task that includes gaining agreement and approval for the process.

2.11.2 Conducting Internal Audits
No Link to Starting Task

Once you have developed your Framework, it is vital to ensure it is being used as intended and that it works properly.

In other words, making sure you actually do what your organisation said it was going to do.

The process for assessing that your Framework does what it says it will do is called an internal audit. An internal audit can either be done in one big assessment or in many smaller assessments that together cover all the activities within your Framework. No matter which way you choose, an audit is something that is repeated at regular intervals.

Your ships will have an ISM Code management system which already includes internal audits. If your organisation has an ISO management system such as ISO 9001, ISO 14001 and ISO 50001, that management system will also include internal audits.

Your ISM Code audit process should include tasks related to:

- How to do the audits, what process to follow, who does the audits, what is their competence and how audit findings are recorded.
- What audit reports should contain including:
  - How to identify which audit findings are critical and which less so.
  - What action to take related to various audit findings.
- Follow up of actions from an audit.

Please use this process as far as possible for the internal audits of your Framework.

Before starting to describe the auditing process, being cognisant of your organisational culture, determine:

- What elements of your Framework you want the internal audit to cover, i.e. determining the audit scope. This would normally be all the activities and processes included in your Framework.
- How to determine how frequently activities in your Framework should be audited. Not all activities included in your Framework have to be audited at the same frequency, so you need a process to determine how often each activity should be audited. Look at which activities are more critical in terms of regulatory requirements, stakeholder demands, environmental aspects and impacts and risks and determine how often each should be audited.
- If certain processes or activities are already included in other audits, check what the scope of these audits is, if there is any overlap between the audits, how frequently they take place, and if it is possible to align audit frequency.

Write down the proposed audit scope and frequency for all the activities covered by your Framework.

A critical question is how your organisation can manage an internal audit when a ship is in port for a very short time, when the team onboard is busy and the auditor has to be independent. You should use a simple approach to onboard audits as it is not affordable to send someone around the world to internally audit every ship. Towards this end, the internal auditor can develop a checklist that is unique for each audit and for each ship and that reflects results from the last audits and ISM Code audits, information on accidents, incidents and reports by Recognised Organisation. This checklist can be passed on to shore-based staff in ports who then work through the checklist and feed their findings back to the internal auditor.

As you might be biased in favour of your Framework, you (or your team) should not perform the internal audit yourself. Instead, the auditor should come from outside the team that built and operates your Framework. This will also give you a fresh perspective on your Framework: a new pair of eyes may see opportunities that you previously might not have seen.

2.12 Advancing: Staying On Track

Advancing Tasks within this area allow you to review how your Framework functions, if it needs to be improved and also to look at how to deal with any errors and near misses that may occur in activities in your Framework.

2.12.1 Identifying, Mitigating And Managing Errors And Near Misses

Linked to Starting Task 2.7.1

Now that your Framework has been operating for some time you can begin to identify near misses in addition to errors that you initiated in Task 2.7.1.

Near misses are errors that have not happened but could have happened if someone had not intervened in time. If you cannot find anything related to your organisation's activities, you could check the newspapers or learn from other people's experience and errors.

For example, if an accidental chemical release into the ocean is reported in the news and you ship chemicals, look at your processes to see if they might need amending based on the learning lessons you can derive from the accident investigation of the incident (if that is available).

Review the process you developed in Task 2.7.1 and add the following information:

- What is a near miss in your Framework.
- How to minimise its impact.
- How to report it and to whom.
- What action to take and what time scale.
- Review near misses to derive learning lessons.

Confirm this process and include it in your Framework

2.12.2 Taking Corrective Action

Any errors or near misses as well as any other failure of your Framework to function as described in an activity/process description or related to objectives, commitments etc. need to be acted on. Such corrective actions are critical to improving your Framework.

You can choose to have a common process for your Framework related to corrective action or you can embed such a requirement in each relevant process. Such a process description includes:

- When action needs to be taken and by whom.
- What type of action needs to be taken. This will depend on the consequence of an error, near miss or failure to meet process requirements, objectives, policy etc.
- Mitigation approaches.
- Effectiveness of action taken.
- How to evaluate the error, near miss or failure to meet a process requirement, objectives, policy etc. and derive learning lessons from it.
- How to establish if there may be other as yet unidentified similar errors, near misses or failure to meet process requirements, objectives, policy etc. in your Framework.
- Determine if changes need to be made to your Framework.

Reviewing And Improving Your Framework
No Link to Starting Task

This task is about taking an overview of your entire Framework and its activities and processes.

The purpose is to assess whether your Framework continues to deliver your organisation's commitments and whether the commitments made remain applicable and feasible.

This review is a strategic review of the total activities and processes in your Framework and should take account of:

- What is the management's intention for your Framework?
- What are the commitments in your Framework policy?
- Is your Framework meeting those commitments?
- What does the information collected and evaluated say about your Framework and its functioning?
- Are any changes on the horizon that may impact your Framework?
- What are the learning lessons from your Framework?
- What needs changing in your Framework?

There is no predefined time frame within which your Framework should be reviewed. This is entirely at your discretion. For many organisations, this is once a year.

Process For Strategic Review
In order to conduct an effective review you need to provide management with succinct information related to questions such as:

- Have your organisation and its activities changed and if so, how and how does this impact your Framework?
- Is the scope of your Framework still applicable to your organisation?
- Are there any emerging regulatory requirements or stakeholder demands that need to be included in your Framework?
- Have the strategic business objectives of your organisation changed and if so, how does that affect your Framework policy or other elements of your Framework?
- Are any changes on the horizon – be they commercial, organisational, financial or regulatory – that may impact the aims of your Framework and resources available?
- What does the information collected and evaluated tell you about:
  - how your Framework is functioning;
  - how it is delivering on its commitment;
  - how it is flagging failure to address changes in regulatory requirements, environmental issues and risks at a stage where such failure can be addressed?
- What have you learnt from audits, errors and near misses?
- Are the processes for addressing audit findings and for mitigating and managing errors and near misses working effectively?
- How are processes functioning? Based on new developments or learning lessons, do any processes need to be updated or amended? Pay specific attention to regulatory requirements, the identification and evaluation of risks, as well as environmental aspects and the evaluation of their significance.
- Can you identify any opportunities for improving your Framework?
- What lessons have you learnt from communication, including what has worked well?

Develop a short summary of the information from the above questions that allows management to review your Framework and hold a meeting with them to:

- Agree any actions resulting from the above information.
- Review commitments and policy and agree any changes as applicable.

Process For Future Reviews

Upon completing your inaugural review, ensure that you describe the process that you followed, the questions that you asked and the management meeting that reviewed the outcome and decided on actions. This will ensure repeatability and consistency in future reviews.

More specifically, describe the process including:

- How to conduct the review.
- How frequently it should be conducted.
- What information has to be provided to management.
- How to highlight critical issues and distinguish them from non-essential matters.
- Who in the senior team reviews your Framework.
- What actions were taken based on the outcome of the review.
- How to communicate the outcome of the meeting (internally).

2.12.4   Checking If Your Framework Is Adding Value

In the previous task, we looked at the formal task associated with a strategic review which tends to focus on how the existing system is functioning but does not clearly ask the critical question - 'is your Framework adding value to your organisation?'

This is not a question you or anyone involved in your Framework can answer, so it is best to ask people removed from it these questions:

1. Has your Framework helped to:
    - Save money?
    - Make regulatory compliance easier and cheaper?
    - Make management of environmental and efficiency issues more streamlined?
    - Reduce risks and in some cases liability?

2. Does your Framework negatively affect the way your organisation carries out its regular business? If so, how and what can be done to prevent or reduce this from happening?

If, based on the responses, you find that your Framework has not lived up to your organisation's expectations in adding value to its business, identify the three most critical issues that need to be improved. Discuss with all relevant staff:

- The issues that have been identified.
- What action has been suggested to alleviate the issues.
- Why you are suggesting this specific action (and not another).
- How the changes can be incorporated into your Framework.
- How they would reduce the negative impacts of your Framework.

Repeat this step at regular intervals and remember to ask staff at various levels in the organisation, possibly anonymously at times.

CHAPTER THREE

CONTENTS

THE GUIDE AND REGULATORY COMPLIANCE

THE GUIDE AND REGULATORY COMPLIANCE

One of the significant challenges for ships, their owners, operators, charterers and managers is how to reduce the risk of non-compliance with regulatory requirements and associated enforcement actions.

This Chapter looks specifically at that issue and at how the Guide supports you in managing the risk associated with regulatory non-compliance.

The potential consequences of non-compliance can be significant. For example, a ship can be detained hence delaying its journey with consequences on delivery dates and charter terms. Minimising the risk of regulatory non-compliance is thus critical. In addition, for a ship, every port State is an enforcement authority.

The previous Chapter (Chapter 2) includes tasks dealing with identifying, managing and evaluating regulatory requirements and compliance.

This Chapter (Chapter 3) focuses on regulatory compliance and enforcement actions. It begins with the issue of policing regulatory requirements – who can check a ship for regulatory compliance - and then moves on to look specifically at Port State Control. The Chapter then presents which issues should be taken into consideration in order to strengthen your Framework's capability to reduce the risk of non-compliance. Finally, the Chapter looks at how your Framework can be used to help manage, if applicable, the Environmental Compliance Plan, a set of obligations commonly applied to ships found in non-compliance with regulatory requirements in US waters.

3.1 Who Is Authorised To Check A Ship For Regulatory Compliance?

In order to ensure that ships comply with regulatory requirements, there are two main control functions as follows:

- The ship's flag State, normally via a Recognised Organisation.
- The port State related to the country where a ship may sail to and from – known as Port State Control (PSC).

Flag States have the authority and responsibility to enforce regulations over ships flying their flag. In many cases, flag States may delegate the verification of regulatory compliance to Recognised Organisations – usually classification societies which survey a ship on a regular basis (typically every 6 months, 2.5 years and 5 years, focusing on different areas onboard).

In addition to flag States, port States also check ships entering their ports for regulatory compliance. PSC is part of an international effort to identify and eliminate sub-standard ships. It is the inspection of foreign ships in other national ports by PSC officers (inspectors) for the purpose of verifying that the competency of the master and officers onboard, and the condition of the ship and its equipment comply with the requirements of international Conventions (e.g. SOLAS, MARPOL) and that the ship is manned and operated in compliance with applicable international law.

Regional cooperation among port States has led to the conclusion of Memoranda of Understanding (MOU). These MOUs seek to promote and realise more effective PSC for a given region and to eliminate the operation of sub-standard ships through a harmonised system of PSC. The basic principle is that the prime responsibility for compliance with the requirements laid down in the international maritime Conventions lies with the ship owner/operator, whereas the responsibility for ensuring such compliance remains with the flag State.

The first MOU was signed in Paris in 1982. Since then, MOUs concerning the implementation of PSC regimes have been concluded in a total of nine regions in the world, as summarised in the following list:

- The Paris MOU (European coastal States and the North Atlantic basin from North America to Europe).
- The Tokyo MOU (Asia-Pacific region).
- Acuerdo Latino or Acuerdo de Viña del Mar (South and Central America).
- The Caribbean MOU (the Caribbean Sea and the Gulf of Mexico).
- The Mediterranean MOU (the southern and eastern Mediterranean region).
- The Indian Ocean MOU (the Indian Ocean region).
- The Abuja MOU (West and Central Atlantic Africa).
- The Black Sea MOU (Black Sea region).
- The Riyadh MOU (Persian Gulf region).

The United States of America are not a member of any MOU and undertake control measures on a unilateral basis. The US Coast Guard (USCG) verifies that all foreign ships operating in US waters are complying with international Conventions, as well as all applicable US laws, regulations and treaties.

3.2 Port State Control – What To Expect And How To Prepare?

In 1995, the International Maritime Organization (IMO) adopted a resolution providing basic guidance on how PSC should be conducted and how to identify deficiencies of a ship, its equipment or its crew. The purpose of this guidance is to ensure that inspections are consistently applied worldwide from port to port and even though it is not mandatory, many port States follow it.

Ships to be inspected are selected from a list of ships arriving in the port, often using statistical techniques to identify higher-risk ships. The Paris MOU, for example, assigns an overall targeting factor to ships, whereas the USCG has developed a boarding priority matrix for the purpose of calculating a targeting factor.

A typical PSC will include the following elements:

- Inspecting the ship's certificates.
- Looking at the ship's condition, equipment and the crew at work.
- Looking at any target areas that the PSC officers prioritise, such as security or pollution.

The inspector will note down any deficiencies found. A deficiency exists when some aspect of the ship does not comply with the requirements of a Convention or other regulatory requirements. In case serious deficiencies are found during a PSC, an expanded examination will be carried out.

The number and nature of the deficiencies found determine what corrective action the ship needs to take and whether or not the ship is to be detained. There are four different corrective actions that an inspector may impose on a ship with deficiencies (in order of ascending gravity):[1]

- Deficiencies can be rectified within a certain specified time limit for minor infractions.
- Under specific conditions, deficiencies can be rectified when the ship arrives at the next port.
- Deficiencies must be rectified before the ship can depart the port.
- Detention of the ship.

In case there are severe deficiencies, an investigation could be started which can target both the company with regulatory compliance responsibility for the ship and the crew onboard. In the United States, for example, presenting log books, Oil Record Books or records with false or incorrect entries, carries severe criminal penalties.

By presenting information on international and regional environmental regulations and providing guidance on how to meet or even go beyond their requirements, this Guide can help crews perform their duties in a way that complies with regulations, thus supporting them should they be subject to prosecution following PSC.

The Box Out on the following page provides further guidance on how to ensure a hassle-free PSC demonstrating compliance with applicable regulatory requirements.

More in-depth guidance on PSC in the United States can be found in the BIMCO publication 'Port State Control Inspections in the USA', provided in Part Three of this Guide (on the USB memory stick supplied) as well as online from BIMCO's website.

10 Top Tips For A Good PSC Inspection

1. First Impressions Have An Impact
Imagine a PSC officer being met at the ship by:
- A dirty or oily gangway.
- A daydreaming watchman.
- Sloppy ISPS procedures.
- A messy deck and accommodation.
- Crew in doubt of their assigned duties.

This could lead to an unnecessary bad start on what could otherwise have been a trouble-free PSC!

2. Make Sure That Procedures Are Being Followed
Once onboard, PSC officers start by checking the ship's certificates. They will want to make sure that the ship has the required certificates, and that they are valid.

Some certificates, such as the International Oil Pollution Prevention Certificate attachments will tell the PSC officer what equipment is onboard, and what related procedures are required. The inspector will focus on such equipment and procedures during his inspections. Safety Management System (SMS) procedures may also be checked. Therefore have all documents ready before the PSC officer arrives.

3. It Is A Crime To Present A Falsified Log Book
Not only can presenting falsified log books be a crime, but so is lying to officials. It can carry severe punishments. Bridge inspections usually focus on:
- Operational equipment.
- Nautical publications, charts and posted information.
- English speaking operator of the radio equipment.
- Officers familiar with the equipment and publications, procedures and requirements in respect of log and record keeping.

Equipment can of course break down or need servicing. Tell the PSC officer upfront and ensure that the logs do not contain incorrect entries.

4. It Is The Checks, Not The Ticks That Count
What is the PSC officer looking for?
- The presence of required equipment.
- The condition of the required equipment.
- The knowledge of the crew in respect of the maintenance and operation of safety equipment and their own duties.
- Evidence that effective safety management and security procedures are in place onboard. Checklists can be found in the ship's SMS – USE THEM, and remember that it is a crime to present a falsified checklist to an official.

5. Housekeeping Counts - Make A Good Impression!
The crew accommodation, including the galley, may not be important from a safety and environmental protection point of view, but the appearance of the accommodation and galley is important, as it is often considered representative for the condition of the ship and the quality of the management onboard. Make sure that fire doors are not forced open by unauthorised means – not even temporarily.

6. Ensure The Engine Room Is A Safe Area
The inspection of machinery spaces concentrates on identifying fire, personal injury, electrical and environmental hazards.

The PSC officer will focus on the awareness of and compliance with the SMS procedures, and the familiarity of the crew with the operation of equipment such as the oily water separator, emergency fire pump and emergency steering. Emergency exits must be unobstructed, well-marked and lit – and they must not be locked, e.g. for security purposes, if that prevents their use.

7. PSC Focus On Environmental Compliance

Inspections are focused on identifying the intentional discharges of oil, and on checking if the crew try to hide violations. When inspecting ships for environmental compliance, the PSC officer often looks for:

- Genuine entries in the logs and Oil Record Book. Entries in the Oil Record Book in line with statements from the crew regarding actual procedures followed.
- Records of operations, maintenance works and malfunctions of the pollution prevention equipment.
- The crew are familiar with their duties in respect of operation of pollution prevention equipment under the SMS.
- Signs of tampering with the piping or the electrical controls on the oily water separator.

8. Evidence Of Compliance - Consistency Counts

The information on the supplement to the International Oil Pollution Prevention Certificate relates to:

- The Shipboard Oil Pollution Emergency Plan.
- The SMS.
- Machinery spaces.

If there are differences between the information on these documents and what is found onboard, you should inform the PSC officer and not wait for him to find out himself! Prepare documentation to show that procedures are being followed. These include records of drills and exercises, the Oil Record Book, and waste delivery receipts. Unofficial logs and records, such as sounding books, are treated as official documents.

9. Prove That You Use The Equipment – The Right Way!

The PSC officer may ask for an operational test of the oily water separator. The tests will seek to confirm the performance of both the oily water separator and the engineers operating the oily water separator. All engineers assigned with operation of the oily water separator should be prepared to conduct such tests.

Close inspection of oil content monitors should be expected. NEVER tamper with this equipment as the PSC officer will be looking for signs of tampering. Equipment performance may also be tested. Tank levels may be checked to confirm that they are in accordance with Oil Record Book entries. In oil content monitors with a data logger facility, the PSC officer may check this information against what has been recorded in the Oil Record Book.

PSC officers may also check incinerators and the standard discharge connection to verify regular use. Any connections, hoses and fittings that can be used to discharge directly overboard will give rise to suspicion.

10. Preparing For Inspections And Co-Operating With The PSC Officer – Do Not Hide Facts

Ensure that all are familiar with their environmental SMS duties. Make sure repairs, adjustments and maintenance cannot be read as "tampering" - and record it in the Oil Record Book immediately.

If dismantling of equipment is required to carry out tests, then label it accordingly. That will reduce the risk of being suspected of tampering. If ship's equipment, such as a hose, is used for discharge to reception facilities, then record it – do not hide it. Keep the spare parts inventory up-to-date. Do not cause unnecessary suspicion by being unable to locate the spare parts.

3.3 Planning To Prevent Enforcement Actions

The US Department of Justice (US DoJ) provides useful information in relation to *'Factors in decisions on criminal prosecutions for environmental violations in the context of significant voluntary compliance or disclosure efforts by the violator'*.

One of the considerations relates to 'Preventative Measures and Compliance Programs' and the US DoJ notes that *"Compliance programs may vary but the following questions should be asked in evaluating any program:*

- *Was there a strong institutional policy to comply with all environmental requirements?*
- *Had safeguards beyond those required by existing law been developed and implemented to prevent noncompliance from occurring?*
- *Were there regular procedures, including internal or external compliance and management audits, to evaluate, detect, prevent and remedy circumstances like those that led to the noncompliance?*
- *Were there procedures and safeguards to ensure the integrity of any audit conducted?*
- *Did the audit evaluate all sources of pollution (i.e., all media), including the possibility of cross-media transfers of pollutants?*
- *Were the auditor's recommendations implemented in a timely fashion?*
- *Were adequate resources committed to the auditing program and to implementing its recommendations?*
- *Was environmental compliance a standard by which employee and corporate departmental performance was judged?"* [2]

Your organisation can use these questions in a preventative manner to ensure your Framework has been built to minimise the risk of regulatory non-compliance. The questions can also be used as part of the tasks of internal audits and reviews in your Framework.

To make this easier, the table on the following page links the topics covered in the questions above with various tasks related to building your Framework. The wording of the questions has been changed to align it with the terms used throughout this resource.

NOTE: Your Framework must consistently and holistically provide answers to these questions. The questions are not exhaustive but examples of topics to be covered.

[2] US DoJ (1991) Factors in decisions on criminal prosecutions for environmental violations in the context of significant voluntary compliance or disclosure efforts by the violator.

Questions To Help Minimise The Risk Of A Regulatory Non-Compliance	Tasks In Chapter 2 That Can Provide Input To Answering The Questions
Is there a strong organisational policy and processes to comply with all environmental requirements?	• 2.4.2 & 2.9.2 Regulatory Requirements • 2.4.6 & 2.9.5 Identifying And Managing Risks • 2.5.5 & 2.10.4 Ensuring Competence • 2.5.6 & 2.10.5 Internal Communications • 2.6.1 & 2.11.1 Collecting Information & Identifying What You Need To Track • 2.7.1 & 2.12.1 Identifying, Mitigating And Managing Errors And Near Misses • 2.10.1 Your Framework Policy • 2.10.8 Emergency Preparedness • 2.11.2 Conducting Internal Audits • 2.12.2 Taking Corrective Action • 2.12.3 Reviewing And Improving Your Framework
Are safeguards, beyond those required by existing law, implemented to prevent regulatory non-compliance from occurring?	• 2.4.2 & 2.9.2 Regulatory Requirements • 2.4.5 & 2.9.4 Identifying The Environmental Aspects And Impacts Of Your Activity And Their Significance • 2.4.6 & 2.9.5 Identifying And Managing Risks • 2.5.5 & 2.10.4 Ensuring Competence • 2.5.6 & 2.10.5 Internal Communications • 2.6.1 & 2.11.1 Collecting Information & Identifying What You Need To Track • 2.7.1 & 2.12.1 Identifying, Mitigating And Managing Errors And Near Misses • 2.11.2 Conducting Internal Audits • 2.12.2 Taking Corrective Action
Are processes in place including internal or external regulatory compliance evaluation and audits, to evaluate, detect, prevent and remedy potential and actual non-compliance with regulatory requirements?	• 2.4.2 & 2.9.2 Regulatory Requirements • 2.4.6 & 2.9.5 Identifying And Managing Risks • 2.5.5 & 2.10.4 Ensuring Competence • 2.5.6 & 2.10.5 Internal Communications • 2.6.1 & 2.11.1 Collecting Information & Identifying What You Need To Track • 2.7.1 & 2.12.1 Identifying, Mitigating And Managing Errors And Near Misses • 2.11.2 Conducting Internal Audits • 2.12.2 Taking Corrective Action • 2.12.3 Reviewing And Improving Your Framework
Are there processes and safeguards to ensure the integrity of any audit conducted?	• 2.11.2 Conducting Internal Audits • 2.12.3 Reviewing And Improving Your Framework
Does the audit scope include the evaluation of all sources of pollution (i.e., all media), including the possibility of cross-media transfers of pollutants?	• 2.4.5 & 2.9.4 Identifying The Environmental Aspects And Impacts Of Your Activity And Their Significance • 2.11.2 Conducting Internal Audits
Does the audit include processes to ensure auditor's recommendations are implemented in a timely fashion?	• 2.11.2 Conducting Internal Audits • 2.12.3 Reviewing And Improving Your Framework
Are adequate resources committed to the auditing programme and to implementing its recommendations?	• 2.12.3 Reviewing And Improving Your Framework
Is environmental regulatory compliance a standard by which employee and corporate departments' performance are judged?	• 2.10.1 Your Framework Policy • 2.12.3 Reviewing And Improving Your Framework

NOTE: These questions are provided by the US DoJ. Other port States' approaches may be different and put the focus on other topics as well as use different language.

3.4　The United States Environmental Compliance Plan

The Environmental Compliance Plan (ECP) is a concept used in the US to ensure compliance with environmental regulations in US territorial waters and comes in two different contexts:

1. **Voluntary ECP:** The voluntary ECP is not based on any specifically imposed obligations or requirements. It is developed and implemented by a company on a voluntary basis to establish company procedures that minimise non-compliance.
2. **Obligatory ECP:** The obligatory ECP may be imposed on a company found in non-compliance with applicable environmental regulations. The USCG determines the specific obligations and requirements for a ship's obligatory ECP on a case-by-case basis.

3.4.1　Voluntary Environmental Compliance Plan

The development and implementation of a voluntary ECP - similar to the development of your Framework - can help shipping companies manage their environmental responsibilities and mitigate the risk of non-compliance. It can be used to demonstrate the company's commitment to compliance, detect non-conformities and correct identified deficiencies.

In addition, from a law enforcement perspective, the existence and adequacy of a voluntary ECP may be considered as a potentially mitigating factor in case the company has been found in non-compliance. The Voluntary Disclosure Policy for environmental crimes cases, issued in 2007 by USCG, essentially states that if a ship owner or operator has previously implemented a Compliance Management System (CMS) to prevent, detect and correct environmental violations and detects and voluntarily reports a violation, the USCG may decide to not refer the matter to the US DoJ for criminal prosecution. This decision depends on whether the voluntary ECP and CMS satisfy the requirements set out in the Policy.

Numerous sources provide guidance on what needs to be included in your organisation's systems and approaches to help reduce the risk of regulatory non-compliance in US waters. The Box Out below provides an example of guidance on developing a voluntary ECP and CMS and their link to the USCG Voluntary Disclosure Policy for environmental crimes cases. This guidance is part of an article published in *Proceedings of the Marine Safety & Security Council, the Coast Guard Journal of Safety at Sea*.

Essential Elements Of A Maritime Environmental Compliance Plan[3]

First, it is important to understand that the CMS discussed in the USCG Voluntary Disclosure Policy for environmental crimes cases is not a substitute for, or an alternative term, to describe a voluntary ECP. CMSs are derived from the general corporate governance responsibilities of corporate officers and directors. An environmental CMS focuses on management's ongoing obligation to clarify the requirements of, and ensure compliance with, applicable environmental standards. It is an important complement to the operational and technical elements of a voluntary ECP. The USCG Voluntary Disclosure Policy highlights six elements deemed critical for a CMS:

1. Compliance policies and procedures that specify how shipboard employees and agents are to meet environmental standards.
2. Assignment of overall responsibility for overseeing compliance with environmental policies and standards, including aboard each vessel.
3. Mechanisms for systematically ensuring that compliance policies are carried out, including monitoring and auditing systems.

---

[3] Linsen, G.F. and Grasso, J.M. (2008) Environmental Imperatives: Essential elements of a maritime environmental compliance plan, Proceedings Winter 2008-09.

4. Communication of the company's standards and procedures to all employees and agents.

5. Appropriate positive incentives to perform in accordance with compliance policies and disciplinary mechanisms for failures to adhere to those policies.

6. Procedures to correct violations and to modify the CMS to prevent future violations.

Second, it is important to note that a CMS alone, even if it tracks each of the critical elements contained in the USCG Voluntary Disclosure Policy, will not be sufficient to satisfy the requirements of this Policy or the broader goal of improving environmental compliance. The CMS must be integrated with a comprehensive voluntary ECP that addresses operational and technical elements required to establish, monitor, and improve environmental compliance.

The commercially-marketed voluntary ECPs, the evaluative criteria contained in the Sentencing Guidelines, and the ECPs associated with recent criminal prosecutions have a number of key elements in common. Although varying in format and complexity, each of these models typically includes the following features:

- High Level Management Oversight.
- Defined Shipboard Responsibility.
- Auditing Processes.
- Technical Requirements - must address the engineering features aboard the vessel that will facilitate compliance with environmental standards and help prevent intentional efforts to circumvent pollution prevention equipment.
- Budget.
- Procedures To Determine Reason For Nonconformity And Ensure Correction.

One additional feature that is found in many of the voluntary ECPs is the need to incorporate management reviews of the ECP and the CMS on a periodic basis, to assess the adequacy and effectiveness of the programme.

How Can This Resource Help?

An organisation that chooses to adopt a voluntary ECP can use the Framework to help develop, implement and maintain the voluntary ECP and CMS. The choice of what to include in its voluntary ECP and CMS is up to the organisation but guidance on what to include is provided in Section 3.3, the Box Out above as well as in the International Safety Management (ISM) Code.

3.4.2 Obligatory Environmental Compliance Plan

This section relates to:

- The ship that is subject to enforcement in US waters and that might be subject to an obligatory ECP.
- The organisation with contractual responsibility for regulatory compliance of the ship above or the organisation that could be deemed to have such responsibility.

When completing Task 2.4.1 'Understanding Your Organisation' in the Framework, you may care to establish if you have ships that enter or may enter US waters and if so, determine who is responsible for regulatory compliance, both under contract and as per US requirements.

What Is An Obligatory Environmental Compliance Plan?

In seeking to change the working practice of those organisations found to be in violation of environmental rules, the US frequently requires adherence to compliance programmes overseen by the courts. Under the 'Environmental Crimes: Voluntary Disclosure Policy', the USCG (on behalf of the US DoJ) can, as part of a plea agreement, impose an ECP on a company that has been found in non-compliance of applicable environmental regulatory requirements. The requirement to develop and implement an ECP is usually in addition to a monetary fine. The performance of a convicted company under the ECP is typically monitored by an external auditor and the prosecuting authority throughout the period of probation.

The aim of an obligatory ECP, when initiated, is to prevent, detect, and remedy any environmental non-compliance aboard the company's ships. It is designed to ensure that an organisation's environmental compliance processes and procedures are understood and adhered to by the crew and shore-based employees at all applicable levels of the organisation.

The scope and complexity of obligatory ECPs have grown substantially over the years to ensure that companies are forced to implement environmental regulatory requirements and formats of ECPs and their requirements may vary widely.

How Can This Resource Help?

An organisation that has been found non-compliant with a regulatory requirement and that is required to develop and implement an obligatory ECP as part of a plea agreement, could choose to use the Framework to help develop, implement and maintain the obligatory ECP and CMS. In such a case, however, the obligatory ECP obligations determined by the court govern what must be done and how.

The Framework and its tasks will have to be adapted to fit the unique obligations relevant in your situation.

CHAPTER FOUR

CONTENTS

THE GUIDE AND MANDATORY INTERNATIONAL INSTRUMENTS

THE GUIDE AND MANDATORY INTERNATIONAL INSTRUMENTS

4.1   The International Safety Management Code

The International Safety Management (ISM) Code became mandatory in 1998. It establishes safety management objectives and requires a Safety Management System (SMS) to be established by the 'Company', defined as

> *"The ship owner or any person, such as the manager or bareboat charterer, who has assumed responsibility for operating the ship."*

The mandatory requirements specified in the ISM Code, if followed and actioned, will ensure that a ship conforms to the provisions of relevant rules and regulations related to pollution prevention, as well as safety issues.

SMS can often be misinterpreted to be solely focussed on safety. This is a common misconception - equal attention should be given to pollution prevention within an SMS.

In summary, the functional requirements of an SMS include the following:

- A safety and environmental protection policy.
- Instructions and procedures to ensure safe operation of ships and protection of the environment.
- Defined levels of authority and lines of communication.
- Procedures for reporting accidents and non-conformities with the provision of the ISM Code.
- Procedures to prepare for and respond to emergency situations.
- Procedures for internal audits and management reviews.

The tasks in the Environmental & Efficiency Management Framework in Chapter 2 can be linked to requirements in the ISM Code related to an SMS as detailed in the table on the next page.

NOTE: The Framework does not set out ISM Code SMS requirements, but describes the tasks necessary to in principle build an ISM Code SMS.

SMS Requirement	Linked Task In Framework
Safety And Environmental Protection Policy	• 2.9.6 Commitments • 2.10.1 Your Framework Policy And inherently input from tasks: • 2.4.2 & 2.9.2 Regulatory Requirements • 2.4.5 & 2.9.4 Identifying The Environmental Aspects And Impacts Of Your Activity And Their Significance • 2.4.6 & 2.9.5 Identifying And Managing Risks
Company Responsibilities And Authority	• 2.4.1 Understanding What Your Company Does • 2.5.5 & 2.10.4 Ensuring Competence • 2.5.6 & 2.10.5 Internal Communications
Designated Person	• 2.5.1 & 2.10.3 Building A Mind Map Of Your Chosen Activities • 2.5.4 & 2.10.9 Pulling It All Together • 2.5.5 & 2.10.4 Ensuring Competence • 2.7.1 & 2.12.1 Identifying, Mitigating And Managing Errors And Near Misses • 2.11.2 Conducting Internal Audits • 2.12.2 Taking Corrective Action • 2.12.3 Reviewing And Improving Your Framework
Master's Responsibility And Authority	• 2.5.5 & 2.10.4 Ensuring Competence • 2.5.6 & 2.10.5 Internal Communications
Resources And Personnel	• 2.5.5 & 2.10.4 Ensuring Competence
Development Of Plans For Shipboard Operations	• 2.5.1 Building A Mind Map Of Your Chosen Activities • 2.5.3 Describing Activities And Processes Covered By Your Framework • 2.5.4 & 2.10.9 Pulling It All Together
Emergency Preparedness	• 2.10.8 Emergency Preparedness
Reports And Analysis Of Non-Conformities, Accidents And Hazardous Occurrences	• 2.6.1 & 2.11.1 Collecting Information & Identifying What You Need To Track • 2.7.1 & 2.12.1 Identifying, Mitigating And Managing Errors And Near Misses • 2.12.2 Taking Corrective Action
Maintenance Of The Ship And Equipment	Embedded in tasks: • 2.5.1 Building A Mind Map Of Your Chosen Activities • 2.5.3 Describing Activities And Processes Covered By Your Framework; • 2.5.4 & 2.10.9 Pulling It All Together
Documentation	Embedded throughout all tasks
Company Verification, Review And Evaluation	• 2.11.2 Conducting Internal Audits • 2.12.2 Taking Corrective Action • 2.12.3 Reviewing And Improving Your Framework

4.2 The Ship Energy Efficiency Management Plan

The International Maritime Organization (IMO) introduced the Ship Energy Efficiency Management Plan (SEEMP) as a mandatory tool under MARPOL Annex VI, entering into force on 1 January 2013. The SEEMP is a management tool that was developed to assist shipping companies in managing the energy efficiency of ships. It sets out a step-by-step framework that ship owners can follow to develop best practice and implement energy efficient operations.

The SEEMP provides a means to formally capture processes by which a ship owner can seek to improve the energy efficiency of operations both onboard each ship as well as organisation-wide. Therefore, the development of your Framework and the development of your SEEMP are closely aligned.

In fact, similarities can be drawn between the steps outlined in the SEEMP and the steps represented within the Environmental & Efficiency Management Framework. Therefore, many of the processes developed for your Framework can be directly transferred into SEEMP subject to a check that the processes are in conformance with SEEMP.

The four steps outlined in SEEMP are briefly outlined below:

1. **Planning**
   As part of each SEEMP, the ship owner is required to review current practices and energy usage onboard each ship with a view to determining any shortfalls or areas for improvement of energy efficiency. This is a crucial first step to developing an effective management plan and should identify various aspect relating to ship-specific measures, company-specific measures, human resource development and goal setting.

2. **Implementation**
   Upon completion of the planning state, a system of how each energy improvement measure is to be implemented needs to be developed. The development of the system can be considered under the planning stage and should set out the actions required to achieve each measure along with who is assigned to them.

   The implementation itself needs to be in accordance with the implementation system and should involve a system of record-keeping.

3. **Monitoring**
   The only way to assess whether the energy improvement measures are working is to quantitatively monitor each one. A ship owner may have existing systems in place to do this, although monitoring should be carried out using established methods, preferably by an international standard.

4. **Self-Evaluation And Improvement**
   This is the final stage in the cycle and is the means by which each measure can be assessed and the results fed into the planning stage of the next improvement cycle. Self-evaluation and improvement not only identifies how effective each energy improvement measure is, but it also determines whether the process by which it is implemented and monitored is suitable and how it can be improved.

   Each measure needs to be evaluated individually on a periodic basis and the results should be used to understand the level of improvements seen for each ship.

The SEEMP should be a 'live' document that is reviewed regularly to establish the relevance and impact of each measure on ship and fleet operations. Again, a similar review process is undertaken through your Framework – further illustrating the case to merge any SEEMP activities into your Framework, or vice versa.

CHAPTER FIVE

CONTENTS

THE GUIDE AND VOLUNTARY STANDARDS AND INITIATIVES

THE GUIDE AND VOLUNTARY STANDARDS AND INITIATIVES

5.1 ISO Standards

Since 1947, the International Organization for Standardization, more commonly known as ISO, has published more than 19,500 international standards.

The international standards are developed by groups of national experts nominated by their National Standard Body. Under ISO Policy, ISO standards must be neutral, voluntary and applicable to all organisations.

International maritime standards are developed under the leadership of ISO Technical Committee 8 which is responsible for the standardisation of design, construction, structural elements, outfitting parts, equipment, methods and technology, and marine environmental matters, used in shipbuilding and the operation of ships, comprising sea-going ships, vessels for inland navigation, offshore structures, ship-to-shore interface and all other marine structures subject to requirements by the International Maritime Organization (IMO). TC8 subcommittee 2 looks specifically at environmental issues such as shipboard garbage, oil spill response, port reception facilities etc.

Examples of ISO standards related to the shipping sector include:

- **ISO 8217:** Petroleum products - Fuels - Specifications of marine fuels.
- **ISO 13617:** Ships and marine technology - Shipboard incinerators - Requirements.
- **ISO 13073:** Risk assessment on anti-fouling systems on ships - Part 1 Marine environmental risk assessment methods of biocidally active substances used for anti-fouling systems on ships.
- **ISO 30000:** Ships and marine technology - Ship recycling management systems - Specifications for management systems for safe and environmentally sound ship recycling facilities.
- **ISO PAS 28007:** Ships and marine technology - Guidelines for Private Maritime Security Companies providing privately contracted armed security personnel.

The Framework in Chapter 2 has been created taking into account developments at ISO related to management system standards, in particular the common framework for management systems that can be found in ISO Directives Part 1 Annex SL. This common framework is being used by many management system standards and is incorporated into the current revisions of ISO 9001, ISO 14001 as well as the new ISO standard on health and safety ISO 45001. The common framework is freely available on the ISO website.

Put simply, a management system helps organisations to establish and maintain a systematic approach to managing their risks and opportunities, be they environmental, related to safety, quality, etc.

We have chosen to use this common ISO approach when developing the Environmental & Efficiency Management Framework.

The Framework can help your organisation implement an ISO based management system. However, you need to make sure you meet all the specific requirements in whatever ISO standard you are planning to implement. The Framework does not include text or requirements from management systems. Choosing to use an ISO based management system standard does not commit you to accredited certification. Conformance to an ISO standard can be demonstrated in several ways, including self-declaration and second or third party assurance.

The table below links the Framework tasks to the associated headings of the common framework for management systems mentioned above.

ISO Common Management System Approach	Relevant Framework Areas And Tasks
Context Of The Organisation	
• Understanding The Organisation And Its Context	• 2.4.1 Critical Starting Point: Understanding Your Organisation And The Bigger Picture • 2.4.2 & 2.9.2 Regulatory Requirements
• Understanding The Needs And Expectations Of Interested Parties	• 2.9.3 Understanding What Your Key Stakeholders Demand And Expect From You
• Determining The Scope Of The Management System	• 2.4.4 & 2.9.1 Determining And Reviewing Which Activities Your Framework Should Encompass
• Management System	• 2.5.1 & 2.10.3 Building A Mind Map Of Your Chosen Activities • 2.5.2 Learning From Existing Processes And Systems Within Your Organisation • 2.5.4 & 2.10.9 Pulling It All Together
Leadership	
• Leadership And Commitment	Indirectly covered in the following tasks: • 2.5.6 & 2.10.5 Internal Communications • 2.9.6 Commitments • 2.12.3 Reviewing And Improving Your Framework
• Policy	• 2.10.1 Your Framework Policy
• Organisational Roles, Responsibilities And Authorities	Indirectly covered in the following tasks: • 2.5.5 & 2.10.4 Ensuring Competence • 2.12.3 Reviewing And Improving Your Framework
Planning	
• Actions To Address Risks And Opportunities	• 2.4.2 & 2.9.2 Regulatory Requirements • 2.9.3 Understanding What Your Key Stakeholders Demand And Expect From You • 2.4.5 & 2.9.4 Identifying The Environmental Aspects And Impacts Of Your Activity And Their Significance • 2.4.6 & 2.9.5 Identifying And Managing Risks
• Objectives And Planning To Achieve Them	• 2.10.2 Objectives

ISO Common Management System Approach	Relevant Framework Areas And Tasks
Support	
• Resources	Embedded in tasks where necessary to ensure sufficient support
• Competence	• 2.5.5 & 2.10.4 Ensuring Competence
• Awareness	• 2.5.6 & 2.10.5 Internal Communications: Raising Consciousness
• Communication	• 2.5.6 & 2.10.5 Internal Communications: Communicating With Individuals Involved In The Development Of Your Framework
• Documented Information: General	• 2.5.3 Describing Activities And Processes Covered By Your Framework
• Creating And Updating Documented Information	Not covered in a specific task but embedded in various tasks
• Control Of Documented Information	Not covered in a specific task but embedded in various tasks
Operation	
• Operational Planning And Control	Operational planning and control is embedded in numerous tasks in Chapter 2 linked to the activities and processes you chose to include in your Framework. Examples include: • 2.5.4 & 2.10.9 Pulling It all Together • 2.10.8 Emergency Preparedness
Performance Evaluation	
• Monitoring, Measurement, Analysis And Evaluation	• 2.6.1 & 2.11.1 Collecting Information And Identifying What You Need To Track
• Internal Audit	• 2.11.2 Conducting Internal Audits
• Management Review	• 2.12.3 Reviewing And Improving Your Framework
Improvement	
• Non-Conformity And Corrective Action	• 2.7.1 & 2.12.1 Identifying, Mitigating And Managing Errors And Near Misses • 2.12.2 Taking Corrective Action
• Continual Improvement	• 2.12.3 Reviewing And Improving Your Framework

5.2 Environmental Evaluation Schemes

There are a number of voluntary environmental evaluation schemes that have been specifically developed for the maritime industry.

Participation in these evaluation schemes can herald many varied benefits for the ship owner or operator.

Some offer financial incentives, such as reduced port dues, others are used by major cargo owners for educated business and chartering decisions. What all of them have in common is that they increase transparency of your environmental credentials which can be used for enhancing reputation.

The scope of the different evaluation schemes varies, with some only covering certain air pollutants, and others extending the scope to include aspects such as waste and chemical pollution. An overview of the main environmental evaluation schemes in operation within the maritime industry is provided in this Section.

The table that follows on the next page shows which environmental aspects each evaluation scheme addresses (organised according to the Chapters included in Part Two of this Guide), its geographical scope, which ship types it applies to and whether or not it provides any financial incentives for participating ship owners and operators. Each evaluation scheme is then briefly described.

5.2.1 Clean Cargo Working Group

The Clean Cargo Working Group is a global business-to-business initiative consisting of leading cargo carriers and their customers dedicated to environmental performance improvement in marine container transport through measurement, evaluation, and reporting.

As part of its objectives, the Clean Cargo Working Group works to collect emissions data annually from its carriers throughout their entire fleet. Shippers receive this data in a scorecard format that highlights average fleet emissions on a trade-lane basis. The group now hosts 40 leading cargo carriers and their customers, representing approximately 85% of ocean container cargo (*accurate at the time of writing: December 2014*).

Through the tools and methodology the Clean Cargo Working Group offers, these companies are increasing the transparency of their environmental performance, which helps them understand and manage their sustainability impacts.

5.2.2 Clean Shipping Index

The Clean Shipping Index is an online tool which gives a rating to ships and shipping companies based on their environmental performance. The index offers environmental ranking for ships and entire carriers based on their performances in five different areas:

- Carbon dioxide.
- Nitrogen oxides.
- Sulphur oxides and particulate matter.
- Water and waste control (ballast water, bilge water etc.).
- Chemicals (antifouling, lubricants etc.).

Ship owners present the environmental profile of their ships or fleet which is then recorded in a database through which the environmental performance of the shipping companies can be assessed. Information within this database can be viewed for a single ship or an entire fleet as well as just a single issue such as waste.

This index is an online business-to-business tool that allows cargo owners to select the cleanest ships and quality operators. Ship owners also use it as a benchmarking tool in order to identify areas for environmental improvement.

	Clean Cargo Working Group	Clean Shipping Index	Environmental Ship Index	Fair Winds Charter	Green Award	Green Marine	Maritime Singapore Green Ship Programme	Shippingefficiency.org
Environmental aspects addressed								
Oily bilge water	■	■			■	■		
Marine lubricants	■	■			■			
Bunkering operations								
Tank cleaning & operational discharge from oil tankers					■			
Garbage	■	■			■	■		
Sewage & grey water	■	■			■			
Transport of liquid chemicals					■			
Carbon dioxide	■	■	■		■	■	■	■
Sulphur oxides & particulate matter	■	■	■	■	■	■		
Nitrogen oxides	■	■	■	■		■		
Ozone depleting substances	■				■			
Volatile organic compounds					■			
Ballast water	■	■			■	■		
Biofouling	■				■	■		
Underwater noise								
Geographical scope								
Global	x	x	x		x			x
Regional				x		x	x	
Applicable ship types								
Container	x	x	x	x		x	x	x
Bulk carrier		x	x	x	x	x	x	x
Tankers					x	x	x	x
General cargo			x	x		x	x	x
RoRo		x	x	x		x	x	x
Cruise		x	x				x	x
Financial incentives associated, e.g. reduced port dues		x	x	x		x		

NOTE: *The table only provides an overview of the different environmental aspects covered, yet other criteria (e.g. safety issues, the existence of environmental management systems) may apply.*

5.2.3 Environmental Ship Index

The Environmental Ship Index, established in 2011, is an international programme developed through the World Ports Climate Initiative of the International Association of Ports and Harbors. The World Ports Climate Initiative seeks international collaboration among ports and shipping lines to further reduce air emissions, greenhouse gases and promote sustainability.

Through the Environmental Ship Index, ports and other interested parties promote ships to use cleaner engines and fuels and receive preferential treatment by allowing discounts on port dues, granting bonuses and other benefits commensurate with the level of cleanliness.

The Environmental Ship Index gives a numerical representation of the environmental performance of ships regarding air pollutants and carbon dioxide. The calculation formula scores nitrogen and sulphur oxide emissions directly and proportionally and gives a fixed bonus for documentation and management of energy efficiency.

The Environmental Ship Index score ranges from 0 for a ship that meets the environmental performance regulations in force to 100 for a ship that emits no sulphur oxide and no nitrogen oxide. By comparing the actual performance of a ship with set baselines, the score can be calculated.

The Environmental Ship Index only includes ships that perform over and above current international legislation (IMO).

5.2.4 Fair Winds Charter

The Fair Winds Charter lays out the industry's commitment to voluntarily switching to low-sulphur fuel while in Hong Kong port. It is a strategic, intentional, and voluntary effort started at the end of 2010 involving many of Hong Kong's leading carriers and cruise liners.

5.2.5 Green Award

The Green Award certifies ships that are clean and safe. Ships with a Green Award certificate reap various financial and non-financial benefits.

At ports in Belgium, Canada, Latvia, Lithuania, the Netherlands, Oman, New Zealand, Portugal and South Africa, the Green Award ships receive a considerable reduction on port dues. Private companies also appreciate the extra quality which Green Award guarantees. Several incentive providers, government institutions as well as private companies grant savings to a ship with a Green Award certificate.

The Green Award certification scheme is open to oil tankers, chemical tankers and dry bulk carriers from 20,000 DWT and upwards, liquefied natural gas and container carriers and inland navigation vessels. The certificate is subject to annual verification and is valid for three years.

5.2.6 Green Marine

Green Marine is an environmental certification programme for the North American marine industry. It is a voluntary, transparent and inclusive initiative that addresses nine key environmental issues. Participants are ship owners, ports, terminals, seaway corporations and shipyards. The cornerstone of the Green Marine initiative is its far-reaching environmental programme, which makes it possible for any marine company operating in Canada or the US to reduce its environmental footprint by undertaking concrete and measurable actions.

To receive their certification, participants must benchmark their annual environmental performance through the programme's exhaustive self-evaluation guides, have their results verified by an accredited external verifier and agree to publication of their individual results.

5.2.7   Maritime Singapore Green Ship Programme

The Green Ship Programme is one of the three programmes under the Maritime Singapore Green Initiative which seeks to reduce the environmental impact of shipping and related activities and to promote clean and green shipping in Singapore.

The Green Ship Programme is targeted at Singapore-flagged ships. The Maritime and Port Authority of Singapore will provide incentives to ship owners who adopt energy efficient ship designs that reduce fuel consumption and carbon dioxide emissions.

5.2.8   ShippingEfficiency.org

ShippingEfficiency.org and the GHG Emissions Rating is an initiative that was launched by the Carbon War Room and RightShip in 2010 with the aim of increasing information flows around the efficiency of the international shipping fleet.

ShippingEfficiency.org enables anyone to tell an efficient, low-emission ship from a less efficient one, for the first time. Using a simple search function, users can pull up an 'A to G' rating for around 60,000 existing ships, including the majority of the world's container ships, tankers, bulk carriers, cargo ships, cruise ships and ferries.

The GHG Emissions Rating is presented using the standard European A - G energy efficiency scale and relative performance is rated from A through to G, the most efficient being A, the least efficient being G. The GHG Emissions Rating Size Group: A - G, are based on the Existing Vessel Design Index (EVDI) Size Score, which indicates the number of standard deviations a ship varies from the average for similar-sized ships of the same ship type.

EVDI values are calculated from ship design information and associated data. The primary sources of this data are:

- RightShip's Ship Vetting Information System.
- Ship owners and operators.
- Yards and engine manufacturers.
- Classification societies.
- IHS Maritime database.

Notes

Please see the Information Librarian for
Leisure and Maritime (ML102) for the USB
memory stick to accompany this book.